Illustrated Guide to
GREAT SMOKY
MOUNTAINS
★ NATIONAL PARK ★

WITH ORIGINAL POSTER ART BY ANDERSON DESIGN GROUP

DANIEL S. PIERCE • JOEL ANDERSON • NATHAN ANDERSON

SPECIAL THANKS TO:

Derek Anderson, Joel Anderson, Kai Carpenter, Aaron Johnson, and Michael Korfhage: for collaborating as a team to create such a beautiful & comprehensive collection of poster art.

Daniel S. Pierce: for providing room & board, guided tours, and for writing the historical content of this book.

Nathan Anderson: for editing Dan's writing, adding creative touches, fun facts and travel tips.

Michael Aday, Librarian-Archivist for the GSM National Park: for your expert advice and photo searching.

Jim Hart, President of Friends of the Smokies and Laurel Rematore, Executive Director and Steve Kemp, Interpretive Products and Services Director at GSMA: for your support in making this book possible.

Proofreaders: Ken Wise, Anne Bridges, Bill Hart, and Geoff Cantrell, Dick Koonce, Dawn Verner
Retired Park Service Consultants: Dale Ditmanson, Bud Cantrell, and Warren Bielenberg
Great Smoky Mountains National Park Staff: Dana Soehn and Jamie Sanders.
Canoe & Fly Fishing Outfitter: David "Fishin' Dave" Pierce **Fish Wrangler:** Evan Gurney

11"x 14" mini prints

18"x 24" gallery prints

postcards

All poster art is available in several sizes including 11" x 14" and 18" x 24" standard frame sizes. We offer postcards, too.

To purchase our classic gallery prints and gifts, please visit:

www.ADGstore.com

Library of Congress Control Number: 2017937221
Second Edition printing: February 2020
© 2020 Joel Anderson. All rights reserved. No portion of this book may be reproduced in any form for any reason without express written consent.

Cover, interior design, and all posters created by Anderson Design Group, Inc.
116 29th Avenue North, Nashville, Tennessee 37203 • Phone: 615-327-9894 • www.AndersonDesignGroup.com • www.ADGstore.com
All photos used by permission. Printed & bound in the U.S.A.

Published by Anderson Design Group, Inc..

Table of Contents

Meet the Creators of this Book...

Photo by Alyssa Adams Palumbo

JOEL ANDERSON *was born in Denver, Colorado in 1965. His family moved every few years to places such as Dallas, Curacao, El Salvador, New York, and South Carolina. Joel studied at Ringling School of Art & Design in Sarasota, Florida where he concentrated on Illustration and Design. After graduating with honors in 1986, Joel moved to Nashville and worked for 7 years at Carden & Cherry advertising agency. While there, Joel won several ADDYS and an Emmy Award for his work on a Saturday morning TV show; independently, he exhibited & sold his paintings in local galleries. Joel co-founded Anderson Thomas Design in 1993 with David Thomas. The firm worked on numerous award-winning projects for clients like Universal Studios, Dream-Works, Hasbro, and Harper Collins. After David retired in 2007, Joel retooled the company as Anderson Design Group and narrowed the focus to illustrative design, publishing and poster art. Joel has published over 1,000 posters and 14 books. One of his most successful projects has been a poster series of all 59 National Parks which spawned his best-selling* 59 Illustrated National Parks *coffee table book, published in 2016.*

"Our posters look old—as if they were produced generations ago. That's because we have spent years studying the rendering techniques, typography, color palettes, and style of art done in the 1920s, '30s and '40s. We create original poster art, but our work is inspired by artists from another era.

As an illustration major in art school, I fell in love with both my wife (who has now inspired me for over 30 years) and with the iconic imagery created during the Golden Age of Poster Art—a glorious early 20th-Century era of commercial art. I was especially captivated by the romance and adventure of travel posters. Back before the age of photography, designers and illustrators used their skills to catch the attention of the viewer, to draw them into a scene, and inspire them to take a trip to some exotic destination. The colors, fonts, and rendering styles were beautiful even though those posters were nothing more than common advertisements created to be pasted up on a wall.

Today, in an era of computerized art, photography and cost-conscious efficiency, our culture craves artistry and craftsmanship. So it's no surprise that we are decorating with yesterday's ordinary advertising art and accepting it as histori-

cal and beautiful—a legitimate, nostalgic, emotionally-engaging art form.

One of my favorite series of prints from the Golden Age of Poster Art was created in response to a crisis. During the Great Depression, the Works Progress Administration sought to help unemployed artists by commissioning posters that would promote the National Parks. I still remember the very first time I saw a WPA print. I was with my son Nathan in the Visitor Center at Yellowstone National Park, and my eye was drawn to a simple yet iconic poster that was screen printed in a limited color palette. I had taken lots of photos, but this poster did what no camera could—it eliminated all the unnecessary details and it focused my attention on the canyon, the majestic waterfall and the open sky above. I immediately bought that poster, and I took it home as a treasured souvenir of the amazing week I spent with my son.

That poster was made possible by seasonal park ranger Doug Leen, who in 1973, found a WPA Grand Teton poster in a pile of trash being hauled out during NPS renovations. He began scouring the country for other surviving prints and negatives. Doug and his team carefully restored and reproduced the 14 designs

they had salvaged, saving the delicate art from extinction, and making fresh reproductions available to the public once more. I will always be grateful to Ranger Doug for having the foresight to hunt down those WPA park posters, and for making the designs available to a new generation. Much of our poster art is a celebration of the WPA style, adapted for today's tastes.

This book is a visual feast for the eyes, combining our original poster designs, oil, digital, and acrylic paintings, with historic and contemporary photos. I had the pleasure of collaborating with a talented team of artists: Aaron Johnson, Kai Carpenter, Derek Anderson and Michael Korfhage—masters at emulating early 20th-Century illustration styles. I am also very fortunate to be able to work with gifted artists who paint with words: Daniel Pierce, a good friend who happens to be a historical expert on all things related to the Smoky Mountains, and my son Nathan, who is an avid hiker, traveler and bon vivant. Between Dan's vast historical knowledge and Nathan's contagious passion for beauty and adventure, I am sure you will enjoy reading this book!"

—Joel Anderson, *Artist, writer, founder & Creative Director of Anderson Design Group*

Photo by Joel Anderson

NATHAN ANDERSON *was born and raised in Nashville, TN. Always ready for a new adventure, he is an avid collector of stories; his nightstand has been hopelessly smothered in books ever since he was a little kid (classics like the Call of the Wild, 20,000 Leagues Under the Sea, and the Three Musketeers are some of his favorites). When Nathan graduated high school, he took a week-long trip with his dad to Yellowstone National Park. Surrounded by the big sky poetry of the West, Nathan discovered his passion for travel writing and the National Parks. He earned an English degree at Lipscomb University and further honed his voice as an apprentice to author Jamie Blaine. In 2013, Nathan joined the family business as a staff writer, customer service specialist, and one-man shipping department. A couple of years later, he took on the formidable task of writing a 400-600 word piece for each of the 59 National Parks in less than 4 months. His resulting body of work was published in* 59 Illustrated National Parks *alongside Anderson Design Group's award-winning poster art. Nathan lives in West Nashville with his wife Kamalani and their daughter Esther.*

"Growing up in Nashville, I never gave much thought to the Smokies. When I wanted to see mountains, my eyes turned West not East. I would think of the tourist traps at Pigeon Forge and sniff. What's

there to do in the Smokies other than putt-putt golf and go-karts? Besides, the Park was far away (3.5 hours, thank you very much) in East Tennessee and what is Clingmans Dome (6,643') in comparison

to Pikes Peak (14,115') or Mount Rainier (14,410')? I just didn't understand what made the Smoky Mountains so Great.

I suppose it's easy to take for granted (and even disparage) what's closest to home. Having met Dan Pierce and seeing the Smokies through his eyes, I realized something: *boy, am I an elevation-snob.* Take my advice, don't let these relatively short mountains fool you. If you're a recovering altitude snoot like me, don't point your nose up at Mount Le Conte and keep looking for higher ground (just give Alum Cave Trail a try, my friend, we'll see who's huffing and puffing). From the bottom of Abrams Creek to the top of Clingmans Dome, this Park is bursting with life. Waterfalls, wildflowers, lightning bugs, salamanders, tuliptrees, mountain farms, scenic trails, black bears, speckled trout, moonshine... now doesn't that sound like a good time?

The following is for those who love the Smokies and for those who haven't yet given them a fair chance. I hope you'll enjoy our tried-and-true travel tips, fun facts, and must-see destinations provided in these pages. I'd venture to say we probably had too much fun putting this book together (the line between work and play blurred beyond recognition after the first few weeks). Ole Rocky Top will do that to you though. It has a way of feeling familiar and brand new all at the same time. There's an old magic in these mountains that enthralls the soul. Come and see."
—Nathan Anderson, *Writer, Traveler, Editor of Anderson Design Group Publications*

Photo by Audrey Keelin

DANIEL S. PIERCE *is an avid hiker, biker, and fly fisherman who has developed an intimate relationship with the Great Smoky Mountains in over fifty years of living on their doorstep. Many of his most memorable experiences with his wife Lydia and their four children have been spent in the Smokies, and all have a special affection for the Cataloochee section. He is one of the foremost experts on the history and culture of the Smokies and is the author of three books on the region:* The Great Smokies: From Natural Habitat to National Park *(UT Press, 2000);* Corn From a Jar: Moonshining in the Great Smoky Mountains *(GSMA, 2013); and* Hazel Creek: The Life and Death of an Iconic Mountain Community *(GSMA, 2017). He also penned the first truly comprehensive history of early NASCAR,* Real NASCAR: White Lightning, Red Clay, and Big Bill France *(UNC Press, 2010) and has appeared in documentaries on the History Channel, CMT, and HBO Canada. He serves as Professor of History, NEH Distinguished Professor in the Humanities, and resident professional hillbilly at the University of North Carolina-Asheville.*

"I first came to Great Smoky Mountains National Park as a three-year-old in 1959 in the midst of a family move from the banks of the Mississippi River in southeast Arkansas to Asheville in the Western North Carolina mountains. My most vivid memory of the trip was the little stuffed black bear I received from my parents which I proudly took to my new home. Growing up, I made many memorable trips into the Smokies hiking, camping, and exploring. I moved away from the region for a few years in the 1980s, but then developed an even deeper connection with the Park when I moved to Knoxville, Tennessee for graduate school in 1991.

When I returned to the area, the Smokies soon became one of the most important places for my wife Lydia and our young family: the site of our first family camping trip, of countless hiking trips, and of innumerable photos destined for our annual family Christmas card. Indeed, Cataloochee has become somewhat of a second home for the Pierce family and camping there in October is an annual, eagerly anticipated, and almost sacred family event.

I also developed a deep professional relationship with the Smokies over those years as I completed graduate school at the University of Tennessee, crossed the Smokies once again, and went to work as a history professor at the University of North Carolina Asheville. The establishment of the Park became the subject of my Ph.D. dissertation and I have since written three books and numerous articles for magazines and newspapers on Smokies-related topics. I also had the privilege of serving two terms on the board of directors for the Great Smoky Mountains Association, working with other Park lovers to educate visitors about the Smokies' natural and human history and distributing millions of dollars in Association revenues to benefit the Park.

In the fall of 2016, my love for the Smokies reaped one of its greatest benefits when I providentially reconnected with artist Joel Anderson, a friend from days living in Nashville in the 1980s. I had not seen or heard from him in more than 20 years, but I accidentally discovered his national park posters and invited him to come to UNCA for a program in celebration of the 100th anniversary of the National Park Service. The result has not only been the rekindling of an old friendship, but a wonderful collaboration on this book with Joel and his son Nathan. As part of that collaboration we have been able to share some magical experiences tramping around the Park, and hundreds of bad puns, while trying to convince our wives that we really were "working."

My goal in providing text for this book is to share with the readers the amazing biodiversity and natural history of this place, the compelling stories of the people (and one dog) who have lived in and visited these mountains, as well as help guide visitors to both well known sites in the Park and hidden gems off the beaten path. In pairing with Joel, Nathan, and the artists of Anderson Design Group, I also hope the reader gets a glimpse of the awe and wonder that the high peaks, the rushing streams, the old-growth forests, the spring wildflowers, and the bountiful wildlife inspire. Most importantly, I hope this book will encourage readers to visit this regional, national, and global treasure even more, to explore it to the fullest extent of their physical ability, and to commit to its preservation for future generations."

—Daniel S. Pierce, *NEH Professor in the Humanities Department of History UNC Asheville*

Photo by Lydia Pierce

18 Foothills PKWY

GATLINBURG ENTRANCE

TOWNSEND ENTRANCE

Sugarlands Visitor Center

LITTLE RIVER

Little River Railroad

Laurel Falls

14

11

HATCHER MTN

COOPER ROAD TRAIL

ELKMONT

13 Synchrono Fireflies

12

BLANKET MTN

The Appalachian Club

LITTLE RIVER

27 Car Camping

28 Backcountry Camping

Cades Cove Loop Road

15

CADES COVE

29 Horseback Riding

27 Car Camping

28 Backcountry Camping

Water-Powered Mills **16**

ABRAMS CREEK

Cades Cove Visitor Center

CADES COVE

ROCKY TOP

THUNDER HEAD MTN

CLINGMANS DOM

APPALACHIAN TRAIL

HANNAH MTN TRAIL

8 Appalachian Trail

Moonshine

JENKINS RIDGE TRAIL

HAZEL CREEK TRAIL

25

26 Fly Fishing

29 Horseback Riding

EAGLE CREEK

28 Backcount Camping

17 Gregory Bald

LOST COVE TRAIL

28 Backcountry Camping

WOLF RIDGE TRAIL

26 Fly Fishing

HAZEL CREEK

HAZEL CREEK

FORNEY CREEK

Backcountry Camping

30 Backcountry Camping

APPALACHIAN TRAIL

29 Horseback Riding

FONTANA LAKE

LAKESHORE TRAIL

29 Horseback Riding

30 Fontana Lake

MAP LEGEND

| ▲ Mountain | **1** Attraction | 🐎 Horse Trail | ········ Trail | — Road | — River | 🌲 Old-Growth Forest |
| ⛺ Backcountry Camping | 🔺 Campsite | Visitor Center | ✹ Wildflowers | 🐟 Fly Fishing | | |

1 US HWY 441	**7** Charlies Bunion	**13** Synchronous Fireflies	**19** Noah Bud Ogle Cabin	**25** Palmer Chapel
2 Mount Le Conte	**8** Appalachian Trail	**14** Little River Railroad	**20** Rainbow Falls	**26** Fly Fishing
3 Alum Cave	**9** Clingmans Dome	**15** Cades Cove Loop Road	**21** Grotto Falls	**27** Car Camping
4 LeConte Lodge	**10** Mountain Farm Museum	**16** Water-Powered Mills	**22** Ramsey Cascades	**28** Backcountry Camping
5 Smoky Jack	**11** Laurel Falls	**17** Gregory Bald	**23** Moonshine	**29** Horseback Riding
6 Chimney Tops	**12** The Appalachian Club	**18** Foothills PKWY	**24** Mount Cammerer Tower	**30** Fontana Lake

Mount Cammerer Tower

23 Moonshine   24

27 Car Camping   **BIG CREEK**

COSBY

27 Car Camping

APPALACHIAN
TRAIL

26 Fly Fishing

OLD SETTLERS
TRAIL

GREENBRIER

MOUNT
GUYOT

MOUNT
STERLING

22

Ramsey Cascades

Noah Bud
Ogle Cabin

MOUNT
CHAPMAN

28 Backcountry
Camping

19

21 Grotto Falls

20 Rainbow Falls

CATALOOCHEE

Smoky Jack 5   2 Mount Le Conte

LE CONTE

1 US Hwy 441   4 LeConte Lodge

3 Alum Cave

28 Backcountry
Camping

Palmer Chapel 25

immey Tops 6

7 Charlies Bunion

29 Horseback Riding

8 Appalachian Trail

Car Camping 27

GARLAND
OUNTAIN
TRAIL

SPRUCE
MTN

26 Fly Fishing

1 US Hwy 441

NEWFOUND GAP

RAVEN FORK

28 Backcountry
Camping

9

ROUGH
FORK
TRAIL

Clingmans Dome
Highest Point in the Smokies

28 Backcountry
Camping

27 Car Camping

27 Car Camping

FORNEY
RIDGE
TRAIL

27 Car Camping

OCONALUFTEE

9 Horseback Riding

26 Fly Fishing

10

NOLAND
CREEK
TRAIL

Oconaluftee
Visitor Center

NOLAND
CREEK

DEEP CREEK

CHEROKEE
ENTRANCE

27 Car Camping

GREAT SMOKY
MOUNTAINS
NATIONAL PARK

★ ADG ☐ USA ★

A Historical Overview of Great Smoky Mountains National Park

IN 1776, naturalist William Bartram first glimpsed the Great Smoky Mountains from the heights of the adjoining Nantahalas and "beheld with rapture and astonishment a sublimely awful scene of power and magnificence, a world of mountain piled upon mountain." Bartram was not the first, and certainly not the last, to stand in awe of this majestic mountain range that by the 20th century would become the most visited national park in the nation, attracting over 10 million visits per year.

The Cherokee, who have probably inhabited the region for over 1,000 years, shared Bartram's awe of the Great Smokies and called them "Shaconage" (pronounced Sha-kon-a-gay), place of blue smoke. The tribe's most sacred site, the Kituah mound, the so-called "Mother Town" of the Cherokee, is located on the edge of the Smokies between the modern-day towns of Cherokee and Bryson City. Many other sites in the region such as Gregory Bald, Andrews Bald, Clingmans Dome, and the Oconaluftee River hold sacred status and appear prominently in Cherokee lore.

The mountains also played more pedestrian roles in Cherokee life, and the biological diversity of the Smokies provided a rich and varied storehouse that supplemented a diet based on the cultivation of the sacred Three Sisters (corn, beans, and squash). While most of their towns were outside the confines of the present-day national park, Cherokee men combed the mountains hunting deer, elk, bear, turkeys, and other game, and fished the streams for native speckled trout. Women made foraging trips into the mountains to gather nuts, berries, medicinal herbs such as ginseng, and river cane for baskets and blowguns. Place names throughout the Smokies (Oconaluftee, Cataloochee, Kanati, and even Cades Cove) reflect the lasting impact of the Cherokee on this region.

Cherokee woman

Great Smoky Mountains National Park Archives

For the Cherokee, the mountains were a place of refuge as well. By hiding out in the vast wilderness of the Smokies, some of the tribe avoided removal over the Trail of Tears to Indian Territory (present-day

> **"The Cherokee legacy is that we are a people who face adversity, survive, adapt, prosper and excel."**
>
> *— Chief Chad Smith (Principal Chief of the Cherokee Nation, 1999 - 2011)*

Oklahoma) in the 1830s. When U.S. soldiers gave up their search for these outliers, the natives were able to join other Cherokee living on land owned by William Holland Thomas, the so-called White Chief of the Cherokee, to form the Eastern Band of the Cherokee Indians.

Through a number of treaties in the early 1800s, the Cherokee lost much of their claim to the Great Smoky Mountains as European settlers moved into the area. While the historical record is sketchy, the first white settler to move into the future park may well have been John Hyde (Hide), who occupied former Cherokee fields on the Oconaluftee River around 1802. Other settlers followed in the early years of the 19th century, settling along streams in the lower, more fertile reaches of the Smokies and eventually reaching some of the large interior hollows such as Cades Cove and Cataloochee. While many of these early inhabitants stayed for only a generation or two before moving west to more fertile fields, others, like the Cherokee, stayed and left their mark on the land; the names of Enloe, Mingus, Oliver, Ownby, Caldwell, Ogle, Oakley, Messer, Oliver, Gregory, Proctor, Cable, and Walker are still common among both place names and family names in the Smokies.

Early settlers lived much like their Cherokee predecessors, cultivating the Three Sisters in river-bottom farms, hunting wild game in the mountains, and gathering nuts, berries, and herbs. The primary differences in lifestyle were the herding of livestock and the various commercial activities the new settlers participated in. Hogs literally ran wild in the forest, fattening on chestnuts, hickory nuts, and acorns, while cattle were driven up to mountain balds to fatten on the rich

A Timeline of the Great Smoky Mountains National Park

The land in the Great Smoky Mountains National Park has been shaped by humans for centuries. The Cherokee people are the earliest known inhabitants and they, like all others who followed, left their marks on the landscape— as have the Spaniards, European settlers, lumber companies, hikers, nature lovers, and tourists who now flock by the millions. This timeline lists some of the significant events that shaped the wilderness and farmland of this national treasure.

1540
Hernando de Soto and force of 620 Spanish soldiers skirt the Smokies

1802
First documented settlement of Europeans in what became the GSM National Park in the Oconaluftee section

1000
First settlement of Kituah, the "mother town" of the Cherokee

1775
William Bartram sights the Smokies and later writes first description of the mountains in English

Typical farmhouse cabin

grasses in late spring. In the fall, cattle, hogs, and even geese and turkeys were driven to market along old Cherokee trails now converted to rough toll roads such as the Cataloochee, Oconaluftee, and Parsons Turnpike.

The settlers also supplemented their subsistence activities by trading items for cash or store credit and by starting small-scale industries. They traded in hides and furs, beeswax, and a variety of herbs. Mills for grinding corn and other grains were profitable enterprises that cropped up in every Smokies community. Some settlers built saw mills or small iron forges and a group of Oconaluftee entrepreneurs formed the Epsom Salts Company and mined Epsom salts at Alum Cave.

Other than livestock, the most common, and probably the most profitable,

commercial activity in the Smokies was the production of corn whiskey. Most families owned a copper forty-gallon pot still where they made liquor for their own consumption, for medicinal purposes, and as a trade item. Some large, strictly commercial distilleries were built in Cades Cove and other areas of the Smokies. Making liquor was perfectly legal up until the passage of the federal excise tax in 1862, but the production of illegal whiskey (called "blockade" or "moonshine") continued as an important economic activity in the Smokies well into the 20th century.

Even as settlers filtered in, the Smokies began to attract elite tourists who came for the spectacular scenery, cool climate, clean air, and healing waters. Resorts such as Montvale Springs, Sulfur Springs, and Warm Springs cropped up in the 1830s on the edges of the Smokies and attracted people from all over the country. Travel writer Charles Lanman came to the Smokies in 1848 and wrote about the beauty of looking down over a Smoky Mountains sunset from Alum Cave and observed, the view "was to me one of the most remarkable and impressive scenes that I ever witnessed…. It was a glorious picture, indeed, and would have amply repaid one for a pilgrimage

from the remotest corner of the earth." With railroads improving access to the area after the Civil War, tourism to such resorts grew and the beauty of the Smokies and the lifestyles of its "strange" mountaineer inhabitants became staples for popular "Local Color" writers like Mary Noailles Murfree.

Elite tourists, however, were not the only outsiders drawn to the Smokies in the late 19th and early 20th centuries.

Captured moonshine still

The mountains increasingly drew the attention of industrialists. The rich hardwood forests of the region were the main attraction. By the 1890s, outside timber companies began extensive splash-dam logging on Big Creek, Hazel Creek, and the Little River. Splash-dam loggers used the power of water to float the more buoyant trees like tuliptrees downstream to mills. Copper deposits in the Hazel Creek and Eagle Creek areas also enticed mining companies who, for a short time, hauled out tons of copper ore.

A full-scale industrial assault on the Great Smokies began in the early 20th century as highly capitalized companies brought steam-powered logging equipment and narrow-gauge railroads to the deepest recesses of the mountains. In the earliest years of the 1900s, large companies like the Little River Railroad

Early mountain settlers

Photos by Open Parks Network

and Lumber Company, Champion Fibre Company, and Ritter Lumber Company launched operations into the remotest coves and the highest peaks of the Smokies. They also constructed huge mills and company towns with hundreds of inhabitants at Townsend, Tennessee and Smokemont, Crestmont, and Proctor in the North Carolina Smokies. By the mid-to-late 1920s, logging company "woodhicks" clear-cut much of the region, hauling out billions of board feet of hardwood and spruce timber. Left behind on the forest floor were the branches and small trees, "slash" in logger parlance, which soon dried and left a highly flammable fuel load. This often combusted into massive forest fires.

Timber companies built a network of railroads to transport logs out of the Smokies

Logging crew

Even as their onslaught on the forests continued, the logging companies unwittingly brought more individuals into contact with the beauty of the Great Smoky Mountains. In the early years of the 20th century, the Little River Railroad and the Oconaluftee Railroad provided weekend "excursion cars" which carried tourists and elite homeowners into the heart of the mountains for day trips and exclusive resort escapades. Some farmers, like John Oliver in Cades Cove, took advantage of the growing attraction of the

Smokies and built tourist cabins on their property. Many of the individuals who were later instrumental in creating the Park got their first exposure to the natural attractions of the mountains this way.

The idea to set aside parts of the Smokies for federal protection first cropped up in the 1890s with mentions in a few magazines and proposals in the U.S. Congress and state legislatures. These efforts never progressed very far. The most substantial early movement was organized in 1899 by Dr. Chase Ambler of Asheville who invited prominent publishers, businessmen, and politicians to gather at the Biltmore Estate to form the Appalachian National Park Committee. The organization soon evolved into a group promoting national forests and responsible timber harvesting, and they changed their name to the Appalachian Forest Reserve Association in 1901. The Great Smoky Mountain National Park dream would lie dormant for another 20 years....

National Parks captured America's imagination in 1916 with the establishment of the National Park Service. Stephen Mather, the first Director of the NPS, was a brilliant promoter of the parks and aggressively advertised the benefits that came to communities surrounding them. In order to expose more

Americans to the national park experience, Mather very much wanted to open parks near Eastern and Midwestern population centers. U.S. Congressmen, seeing the benefits parks would bring to their states, flooded Congress with bills to procure new ones.

In the Smokies region, this movement coincided with increasing concern over the clear-cutting of the mountains. In 1919, North Carolina writer Horace Kephart and Tennessee civic booster Paul Fink began discussing the possibilities of a park in the Smokies, a place where both

Railroad travel brochures

had spent considerable time hiking, camping, fishing, and hunting. Kephart, who believed the mountains had saved him from a life wracked by depression and alcoholism, hated the destruction he was witnessing firsthand. "I owe my life

Timeline of the Great Smoky Mountains National Park

1899
Appalachian National Park Association organized in Asheville, NC

1904
Horace Kephart arrives in Hazel Creek

1910
Appalachian Club resort community at Elkmont established

1913
Our Southern Highlanders first published

1921
European wild boars escape from hunting preserve on Hoopers Bald near Smokies

1923
Smoky Mountains Conservation Association (Knoxville, TN) formed to promote establishment of national park in the Smokies

1901
Construction begins on first railroads into the Smokies (Little River Railroad & Lumber Co. and North Carolina Land & Timber Co.)

1911
Wonderland Hotel built at Elkmont

1916
National Park Service is established

1924
• Smoky Mountains Hiking Club begins clearing for the Appalachian Trail through the Smokies
• National Park Service creates Southern Appalachian National Park Committee

to these mountains and I want them preserved that others may profit by them as I have," he said. Fink encouraged Kephart to use his influence as a nationally recognized outdoor writer to promote the idea of a park in the Smokies, but Kephart foresaw major hurdles. In 1920, he wrote to Fink, "I wish from my heart that I could encourage you in starting a propaganda to have the Government buy up the best forests here before they are destroyed, but there is no hope."

Kephart, however, underestimated both the salesmanship of Stephen Mather, and the economic boosters in Knoxville and Asheville who saw a Great Smoky Mountains National Park as a means of economic salvation for their communities. In order to both promote the idea of parks in the east, particularly

Stephen Mather

the Southern Appalachian region, and gain control of the flood of unsolicited bills for eastern national parks, Mather created the Southern Appalachian National Park Commission. He appointed this blue-ribbon committee of prominent individuals to determine what sites in the region were most deserving of national park status.

In response, individuals and groups in

Asheville, Knoxville, and other regional cities began lobbying the SANPC for their favored sites. Knoxville natives Anne and Willis P. Davis, who had visited the western parks in 1923, became early proponents for a Smokies national park and solicited the help of local booster David Chapman. Chapman would become the long-term and highly energetic leader of the park movement in East Tennessee. North Carolinians were not as unified behind a single site, but boosters there were excited about the prospects of a park somewhere in Western North Carolina. In the summer of 1924, boosters eagerly greeted the SANPC as they traveled through the region visiting potential national park sites.

In December 1924, the SANPC issued its findings. The beginning of the report brought elation to Smokies boosters when it asserted, ". . . the Great Smoky Mountains easily stand first because of the height of the mountains, depth of the valleys, ruggedness of the area, and the unexampled variety of trees, shrubs, and plants." However, the committee named the Shenandoah Mountains of Virginia as the "outstanding and logical place" for a national park due to easier accessibility to the nation's population centers. Regional boosters and politicians persisted and put considerable pressure on Mather. One month later, Secretary of the Interior Hubert Work called on Congress to approve both Shenandoah and the Smokies as potential national park sites. In 1926, Congress did just that.

While Park boosters in East Tennessee and Western North Carolina celebrated the so-called Park Bill, they faced an unusual test since Congress had long declared they would not purchase land for national parks. In the case of Shenandoah and the Smokies, the states were

Horace Kephart

required to purchase the land and then donate it to the federal government. In order to become an official park, Tennessee and North Carolina had to purchase at least 427,000 acres at an estimated cost of $10 million.

Even before passage of the Park Bill, boosters in Knoxville and Asheville launched a fundraising campaign in the fall of 1925 with the goal of securing $1 million for the project. The campaign reached out to elite bankers and busi-

"The nation behaves well if it treats the natural resources as assets which it must turn over to the next generation..."
— *Theodore Roosevelt*

nessmen but also cast a wide net with publicity campaigns among working people and even school children who donated their pennies, nickels, and dimes. The message consistently focused on the economic benefits a Park would bring to the region. As Knoxville Park booster Cowan Rodgers put it, if a national park came to the Smokies, "millions will annually come through our gates and scatter the golden

1925
The chestnut blight first arrives in the Smokies

1925
Tennessee State Legislature approves purchase of 78,000 acres from Little River Lumber Co. for park purposes

1926
• NC General Assembly approves $2 million and TN Legislature approves $1.5 million in bonds for purchase of land for Smokies national park
• Jack Huff opens LeConte Lodge.

1926
The U.S. Congress approves the Great Smoky Mountains as potential national park site

1927
Charlies Bunion created after torrential downpour in Smokies

1928
John D. Rockefeller, Jr. donates $5 million for purchase of park land in memory of his mother Laura Spelman Rockefeller

1930
John Needham and Phillip Hough arrive as first rangers in the Smokies

1931
Purchase of largest piece of property in the Smokies—92,814 acres from Champion Fibre Co.—approved

Magnificent old-growth trees

and Eastern North Carolina. One Tennessee legislator called the project a "fairy dream on a goat hill." However, Park supporters overcame opposition and the bond bills passed, although many people doubted the required $10 million would ever be raised.

Park proponents now faced the daunting task of raising an additional $5 million with few prospects in sight. Arno Cammerer, assistant director of the National Park Service, was asked to solicit large donations from wealthy Americans. His initial attempts to interest Henry Ford and the Vanderbilt family foundered, but in 1928 he hit the jackpot when he took a stack of Thompson and Masa photos to a meeting with John D. Rockefeller, Jr. Rockefeller had already made significant donations for national parks, and pledged $5 million in honor of his Mother Laura Spelman Rockefeller.

While Park boosters celebrated once again, the work of creating Great Smoky Mountains National Park had only just begun. The next major task came in purchasing the land from lumber companies who owned most of the needed property and were unwilling to sell. Buying up their woodlands required extensive condemnation proceedings, many of which dragged on into the late 1930s.

The most dramatic and wrenching aspect of this process came in condemning individual farms and removing the more than 4,000 people living within the proposed Park boundary. While some families unsuccessfully fought removal in the courts, most lacked the resources to hire lawyers and were forced to sell out. By the late 1920s and early 1930s, the sad sights became common: families packed up their belongings and moved out of the coves

and hollows where their ancestors had lived for generations. Some residents were able to stay on their land with annual leases (Lem Ownby, the last leaseholder, stayed on near Elkmont until he died in 1984) but the limitations imposed by the Park Service made leasing not a viable option for most families. As writer and Smokies native Florence Cope Bush observed, "We were given visitors' rights to the land- to come and look, but not to stay."

In the early 1930s, the National Park

Settlers before being removed from the Park

Service began forming a national park on the land as it was purchased. John Needham and Phillip Hough arrived as the first rangers in 1930 and Ross Eakin was named the Park's first superintendent in 1931. In 1934, Eakin hired Arthur Stupka, the Park's first naturalist, and as a result of the New Deal, the Civilian Conservation Corps established the first of twenty-two camps in the Smokies. The young men of the CCC left a lasting impact on the Smokies, building much of the Park's infrastructure during the 1930s. CCC employees Hiram Wilburn

sheckels in our midst."

Boosters did not totally ignore the beauty of the Smokies, however, and took advantage of the considerable talents of Knoxville photographer Jim Thompson, Bryson City writer Horace Kephart, and Asheville photographer George Masa, a Japanese immigrant. All three played key roles throughout the campaign in raising local awareness and demonstrating to a national audience that the Smokies met the high standards for scenic beauty expected of American national parks.

By late 1926, Park boosters had reached their $1 million pledge goal and convinced the legislatures of both states to issue bonds for land purchases worth $4 million. The bond bills faced staunch opposition from timber company lobbyists and apathy or downright hostility from legislators from West Tennessee

Timeline of the Great Smoky Mountains National Park

1931
Ross Eakin arrives as first superintendent of the Park

1934
• First of 22 Civilian Conservation Corps camps established
• Arthur Stupka arrives as first GSMNP naturalist

1935
Newfound Gap Road completed, connecting Gatlinburg, TN and Cherokee, NC through the heart of the park

1936
Blue Ridge Parkway, which would connect Great Smoky Mountains and Shenandoah National Parks, is approved by Congress

JUNE 15, 1934
Congress officially recognizes the Great Smoky Mountains as a national park

1935
Clingmans Dome Road completed, bringing visitors to within one mile of its summit

1937
Mount Cammerer Lookout Tower constructed by CCC

FDR at Park Dedication, 1940

and Charles Grossman also began collecting artifacts of pioneer life for a potential museum from those being removed from the area. Congress officially designated the Great Smoky Mountains as a national park in 1934. With the completion of Newfound Gap Road and the drive from Newfound Gap to Clingmans Dome, car-happy visitors began flooding in. On September 2, 1940, President Franklin D. Roosevelt stood at a rock platform built by the CCC at Newfound Gap to officially dedicate the Park.

World War II brought a major addition

> **"There is nothing
> so American as our
> national parks."**
> *— Franklin D. Roosevelt*

to the Park of almost 46,000 acres on the north shore of the Little Tennessee River when the Tennessee Valley Authority closed the flood gates on the Fontana Dam, cutting off road access to homes in the area. Like their compatriots in Cataloochee and Cades Cove ten years earlier, the inhabitants of Hazel Creek and other North Shore communities had their land

condemned and were forced to move out.

In the post-World War II era, with the increasing availability of automobiles and improved roads, the Smokies saw a dramatic increase in tourism as more and more Americans came to experience the beauty and magic of the mountains. This flood of new visitors soon overwhelmed Park facilities. National Parks all over the nation were experiencing many of the same pressures so in 1955, the National Park Service launched its Mission 66 program to improve visitor facilities and access to all parks by their 50th anniversary in 1966. Mission 66 greatly impacted the Park with construction of new and updated campgrounds and picnic areas, a new visitor center at Sugarlands, a new modern observation tower on Clingmans Dome, and five miles of road into the North Shore section of the Park above Bryson City, North Carolina.

With the rise of the environmental movement, the National Park Service began more ecologically sensitive management of the Smokies. Superintendent Boyd Evison led the way despite criticism from many long-time Park visitors. Evison cut off motorized vehicle access to several miles of primitive roads. The Park Service also installed stronger bear-proof trashcans at campgrounds, picnic areas, and overlooks. This consigned panhandling bears to the backcountry and angered many tourists who counted on seeing a bear when they visited. Even more controversially, the Park Service, facing environmental concerns and huge cost estimates, gave up its efforts to complete the North Shore Road connecting Fontana Dam and Bryson City.

By the end of the 20th century, the Park had received two important designa-

tions recognizing the amazing biodiversity of the Smokies and its international ecological importance. In 1983, the United Nations Educational, Scientific, and Cultural Organization named the Park as a World Heritage Site, "one of the most ecologically rich and diverse temperate zone protected areas in the world." Five years later, the Southern Appalachian Man and Biosphere Project named the Great Smokies as an International Biosphere Reserve. In order to catalog the biological diversity of the Park, Discover Life in America launched its All Taxa Biodiversity Inventory in 1999. The ATBI is an on-going project

The National Park dream becomes a reality

which seeks to identify and catalog every plant and animal species in the Smokies. It has already documented over 18,000 species, several of them new to Park naturalists and/or to science-at-large.

Managers in the Great Smokies also began a series of wildlife restorations and re-introductions to the Park. In 1978, fishery biologists pushed to restore brook trout to the mountain streams with highly successful results. Other species that had disappeared due to overhunting and habitat loss have found rebirth in the Smokies. Peregrine falcons were reintroduced to several sites in the Park in 1984 with subsequent introductions of river otters and red wolves. While the red wolf program was unsuc-

1944
• Congress approves plans for Foothills Parkway
• Fontana Dam completed, adding 45,902 acres to the Park

1957
Construction begins on the Gatlinburg Spur, first section of Foothills Parkway

1960
Construction begins on the North Shore Road through the Park, proposed to connect Bryson City and Fontana Dam

SEPT. 2, 1940
President Franklin D. Roosevelt officially dedicates Great Smoky Mountains National Park at Newfound Gap

1953
Mountain Farm Museum opens at Oconaluftee

1955
National Park Service Mission 66 program begins, results in construction of many Park structures including the Sugarlands Visitors Center and the Clingmans Dome Tower

1958
First documented arrival of the balsam wooly adelgid in the Park.

Park visitors gathering to watch a bear eat left-over picnic food and garbage

cessful, the others have begun to produce viable populations.

The most successful and most popular of these re-introductions occurred in 2001 when NPS transported twenty-five elk to the Cataloochee area of the Smokies. An additional twenty-seven were imported from Canada the next year. The elk have thrived and expanded their range, particularly into the Oconaluftee area. The elk put on quite a show for visitors in the spring when newborn calves

---

"National parks are the best idea we ever had."
— *Wallace Stegner*

---

frolic in the meadows and when the bull elk battle for dominance in the fall, their eerie bugles echoing through the valleys.

While there is much to celebrate in Great Smoky Mountains National Park, there are also many challenges. Partly because of its unique status as a gift from the States of Tennessee and North Carolina, the Park charges no entry fee. This

fact combined with very flat Congressional budget appropriations has created a huge maintenance backlog that runs into the tens of millions of dollars. In addition, the Park boundary does not protect the Smokies from poor air quality and invasive species.

These challenges highlight the need for those who visit, use, and love Great Smoky Mountains National Park to share in the responsibility to protect it and see that the National Park Service continues to provide for the Park's needs. Fortunately, the Park has two non-profit cooperating associations who work tirelessly to both promote and materially provide for its interests. The Great Smoky Mountains Association encourages "greater public understanding and appreciation [of the Park] through education, interpretation and research." Through its sales of educational publications and materials, GSMA has provided over $32 million to support Park educational and research programs, including the donation of the building for the Oconaluftee Visitors Center.

The Park also has a very effective fundraising arm working on its behalf in the

Friends of the Smokies. Founded in 1993, donations by the Friends topped $50 million in 2016, including key financial support for elk re-introduction, a $1.2 million donation towards construction of a new NPS Collections and Preservation Center, and creation of the "Trails Forever" endowment fund.

When Congress passed the National Park Service Organic Act in 1916, it charged the agency with the awesome responsibility of conserving "the scenery and the natural and historic objects and the wild life" of the national parks and to leave them "unimpaired for the enjoyment of future generations." When Congress passed this bill, American citizens and visitors from around the world took on a share of that responsibility. We are to not only enjoy the Park for ourselves, but to see that "future generations" can share the "rapture and astonishment," the "magnificence" of "a world of mountain piled upon mountain" as witnessed by William Bartram in 1775, the Cherokee for over one thousand years, and the millions of people who continue to flock to this incredible place each year.

Photos by Open Parks Network

Black bear cub practicing climbing skills

Timeline of the Great Smoky Mountains National Park

1970
Construction of North Shore Road ends in the completion of six miles of road culminating in a 1,200-foot tunnel, the so-called "Road to Nowhere"

1974
Superintendent Boyd Evison orders installation of "Boyd Boulders" to limit vehicle access to backcountry roads in the Park

1976
Introduction of effective bear-proof trashcans along Park roads and installation of "bear poles" at backcountry campsites

1977
North Shore Cemetery Association formed to advocate for better care of Park cemeteries and for completion of the North Shore Road

1978
Brook Trout Management Plan begins to restore native trout to their traditional habitat

1984
First wildlife re-introduction program in the Park—Peregrine falcons—begins

Since 1953, Great Smoky Mountains Association has supported the preservation of Great Smoky Mountains National Park by promoting greater public understanding and appreciation through education, interpretation, and research. As a non-profit organization, GSMA has provided more than $34 million to the national park primarily through visitor center sales of ranger-approved educational products and membership dues. Call toll-free 888.898.9102.

Make a gift or become a member today at:
www.SmokiesInformation.org

Photo by Jim Mowbray

Whatever you love about Great Smoky Mountains National Park, being a Friend of the Smokies makes it better. Whether it's hiking more than 800 miles of trails, fishing in crystal clear streams, enjoying bears and elk in their natural habitat, or exploring the park's historic cabins and churches, we are proud to support America's most-visited national park thanks to your donations.

Make a gift or become a member today at:
www.FriendsOfTheSmokies.org

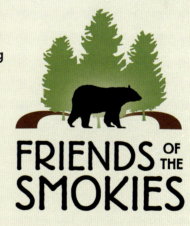

FRIENDS OF THE SMOKIES

1992
Wonderland Hotel Closes for good

1993
Friends of the Smokies formed

1999
All Taxa Biodiversity Inventory to identify and document all biological species in the Park begins

1999
The last remaining leaseholder in the Park, Kermit Caughron, dies

2001
Last leases end for Elkmont summer home owners

2001
First 25 elk reintroduced to the Cataloochee section of the Park

2002
First documented case of hemlock wooly adelgid in the Park

2009
Park celebrates its 75th anniversary with Knoxville Symphony performance in Cades Cove and rededication ceremony featuring Dolly Parton at Newfound Gap

2011
New Oconaluftee Visitor Center funded by Great Smoky Mountains Association and Friends of the Smokies opened

2016
100th Anniversary of the National Park Service

GATLINBURG
ENTRANCE

Sugarlands
Visitor Center

1 US Hwy 441

LE CONTE

Smoky Jack **5**   **2** Mount Le Conte

4 LeConte Lodge

3 Alum Cave

7 Charlies Bunion

Chimney Tops **6**

8 Appalachian Trail

NEWFOUND GAP

1 US Hwy 441

CLINGMANS DOME

9 Clingmans Dome
Highest Point in the Smokies

Mountain Farm Museum   **10**

OCONALUFTEE

Oconaluftee
Visitor Center

CHEROKEE
ENTRANCE

PART 1   *The Heart of the Park*

Newfound Gap Road Corridor (Gatlinburg to Cherokee)

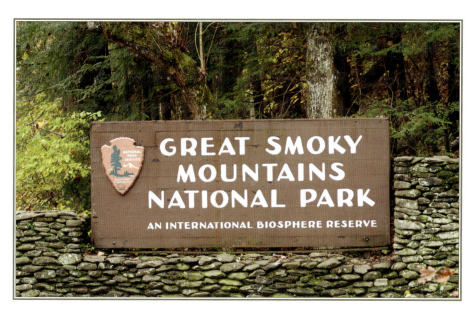

STRETCHING FROM Gatlinburg in the north to Cherokee in the south, Newfound Gap Road (U.S. Highway 441) and its environs comprise the very heart of Great Smoky Mountains National Park. One seeking to drive up, over, and through the Smoky Mountains can do so here, but he won't be alone. More visitors by far enter the Park from the Gatlinburg entrance on US-441 than any other. This section of the Park contains some of the most iconic, and most visited, sites in the Smokies.

Traveling south from Gatlinburg, massive Mount Le Conte greets the visitor as it dominates the viewscape on the first part of the drive. This Southern sentinel beckons many a hardy soul to hike up one (or all) of its six steep trails to the summit. Those with an extra spring in their step may choose to take Alum Cave Trail to Cliff Top (6,555 ft.), where the rustic LeConte Lodge provides a well-deserved bed and hot meal (by reservation only).

The first notable stop on US-441 is Sugarlands Visitor Center, a great place to get oriented to the Smokies. Peer into the Park's human history as young forest slowly reclaims what once was a small farm town in Sugarlands Valley. Car-cramped families can stretch their legs on the Sugarlands Valley and Fighting Creek Nature Trails before heading up the winding mountain highway.

Next, the Chimney Tops Picnic Area is a wonderful spot for rock-hopping in the Little Pigeon River. Those who prefer to keep their feet dry should meander down Cove Hardwood Nature Trail. This walk is especially lovely in the springtime as a parade of kaleidoscopic wildflowers dance across the forest floor. Fearless and properly-shoed individuals will get a kick climbing up to the jagged Chimney Tops, one of the steepest trails in the Park.

History buffs will enjoy Newfound Gap with its massive stone platform where President Franklin Delano Roosevelt dedicated the National Park in 1940. Access to the Appalachian Trail and the glorious overlook atop Charlies Bunion begins here as well.

At 6,643 feet, Clingmans Dome is the roof of the Smokies. Anyone may drive up to within a half-mile of the Dome's observation tower via the skyline drive off of US-441, so long as they visit between April 1st and November 30th (weather permitting).

Elk herds and weary travelers wander the charming Oconaluftee area. A visitors center, the Mountain Farm Museum, and the Mingus Mill all deserve inspection and enjoyment before exiting the Park.

Whether high in the mountains or low in the valleys, spectacular views await those that cross the Smokies on Newfound Gap Road. While the distance between Gatlinburg and Cherokee is only 35 miles, a person can spend a lifetime exploring the heart of the Park's many treasures.

Photo by Joel Anderson

Newfound Gap Road (US Hwy 441)

ONE OF THE GREAT scenic drives in the National Park System, Newfound Gap Road traverses Great Smoky Mountains National Park from north to south. The road connects the gateway communities of Gatlinburg, Tennessee and Cherokee, North Carolina and travels through the very heart of the Park. Much of its route follows the West Prong of the Little Pigeon River in Tennessee and the Oconaluftee River in North Carolina. The upper parts of this scenic drive near the Tennessee/North Carolina line are notable for spectacular views from overlooks along the way. The road also provides access to some of the most popular hiking trails, picnic areas, campgrounds, and historic sites in the Park while giving a unique driving experience with picturesque stone bridges and tunnels and a 360° loop on the Tennessee side.

Much of the road's route follows an ancient trail traveled by the Cherokee and their ancestors to access hunting and gathering sites and connect them to fellow tribesmen across the mountains. Early pioneers converted the route to the Oconaluftee Turnpike, a rough toll road used to drive livestock to market. During the Civil War, Confederate forces improved the road. Soldiers and

Great Smoky Mountains National Park Archives

raiders from both sides used it to move troops and raid enemy communities. After the war, the road languished and fell into disrepair until the 1920s when increased interest in automobiles and in visiting the Smokies prompted the states to improve it. In 1932, the new highway was re-routed into its current configuration that travels over Newfound Gap (the lowest mountain gap in the area) instead of its traditional route over Indian Gap. During the 1930s, WPA and Civilian Conservation Corps workers did much to beautify and improve the road, paving it and adding attractive rock faces to bridges and tunnels.

The road tops out at 5,049 feet in elevation at Newfound Gap, almost midway between Gatlinburg and Cherokee. The parking area at the Gap is crowned with a distinctive stone platform, constructed by the CCC, where President Franklin D. Roosevelt dedicated the Park in 1940. Just past Newfound Gap, the highway intersects Clingmans Dome Road, a scenic skyline drive that takes visitors to within a half-mile of the top of the highest peak in the Smokies.

While the distance between Gatlinburg and Cherokee along Newfound Gap Road is only 34.6 miles, don't expect to get between the two points quickly. The road is heavily traveled; this is a scenic drive with lots to see and experience. So take your time and enjoy the view. The road provides the elderly, young children, and those with physical disabilities unprecedented access to Great Smoky Mountains National Park. But for those with the physical ability to hike just a few miles on a trail, hop a rock, or wade in a stream, Newfound Gap Road provides an introduction and a gateway to years worth of memorable and life-changing adventures.

EXTRAS

⭐ **JUST FOR FUN:** Stand in two states (TN & NC) at once near the Newfound Gap parking lot.

ℹ **DID YOU KNOW?** Even on the hottest summer days, Newfound Gap is around 10-15° cooler than the valley floor.

🚗 **ROAD TRIP TIP:** US Hwy 441 runs from Rocky Top, TN all the way down to sunny Miami, Florida. That's 939 miles of old southern highway.

Look for **FRASER FIR TREES**

HIGHWAY 441 18" x 24" Poster art created in 2017 by Aaron Johnson & Joel Anderson >

© 2017 Anderson Design Group, Inc. All rights reserved.

MT·LeCONTE

GREAT SMOKY MOUNTAINS

CARLOS C. CAMPBELL
OVERLOOK

Mount Le Conte

Photo by Joel Anderson

"**THE CROWN JEWEL** of the Great Smoky Mountains" is Mount Le Conte, proclaims author Ken Wise. Many observers have agreed over the years and the view of Le Conte looming over the eastern gateway to the Park at Gatlinburg is one that visitors will never forget. While at 6,593 feet its peak is not the highest in the Park (it ranks third behind Clingmans Dome and Mount Guyot), its massive size and dramatic 5,301-foot rise from its base near Gatlinburg make it one of the most spectacular sights in the whole eastern United States.

Although the views of Le Conte from Newfound Gap Road, the Gatlinburg By-Pass, or from Gatlinburg's Ski Mountain are breathtaking and unforgettable, Mount Le Conte is best experienced from its six different trails (Alum Cave, the Boulevard, the Bullhead, Rainbow Falls,

Trillium Gap, and Brushy Mountain) that lead to its summit. Each affords its own rewards. The shortest route to the top of Le Conte is along Alum Cave Trail, a sometimes-steep 5.1 mile trek. The longest is the Boulevard Trail which stretches 8.2 miles from Newfound Gap to the summit. Along all six trails the visitor can experience quiet streamside walks through cove hardwood forests, waterfalls, wildflowers carpeting the forest floor in spring and summer, scrambles over rocky pinnacles, and spectacular views of surrounding valleys and peaks. A forest of red spruce and Fraser fir - more typical of Canada than of the Southeast United States - covers most of the summit.

Mount Le Conte actually has five different peaks (West Point, High Top, Cliff Tops, Myrtle Point, and Balsam Point),

each with its distinct views and pleasures. Myrtle Point is generally regarded as the best site in the Smokies to witness a sunrise. On a clear day the sun rises over the Black Mountains sixty miles away and progressively bathes Mount Sterling, Mount Guyot, Charlies Bunion, the Sawteeth, and Mount Kephart in morning sunlight. The Huber's sand myrtle that grows in the area displays beautiful pink and white blooms in June and gives the site its name. Cliff Tops is a great place to catch the sunset over Chimney Tops, Mount Mingus, and Clingmans Dome.

The summit also offers the only lodging inside the Park at LeConte Lodge, a site that has welcomed visitors since 1925. There is also a backcountry trail shelter near the top available to backpackers by reservation.

EXTRAS

⭐ **JUST FOR FUN:**
Cool off beside the 80-foot Rainbow Falls on your way up to the top of Mount Le Conte. In the winter, long cold spells can cause this waterfall to freeze up into a glistening hourglass shape.

ⓘ **DID YOU KNOW?**
The LeConte Lodge staff employs sure-footed llamas to carry supplies up to the Lodge via Trillium Gap.

Look for the
PILEATED WOODPECKER

‹**MOUNT LE CONTE** 18" x 24" Poster art based on a digital painting created in 2017 by Aaron Johnson

Alum Cave Trail

GREAT SMOKY MOUNTAINS
NATIONAL PARK

Alum Cave

A MUCH-LOVED HIKE in the Smokies is the 2.2 mile climb up to Alum Cave. The site is not actually a cave but a huge bluff, or ledge, of black slate jutting out from the side of Peregrine Peak. The slate has traces of iron sulfide which slowly eat away at the rock and create a layer of dust on the "cave" floor. Miners once filled wagons with piles of alum here, and visitors can still catch a whiff of the sulfur in the rock and in the air as they explore the area below the bluff.

Alum Cave has attracted visitors for many years and a Smokies legend asserts that it was "discovered" by Cherokee Chief Yonaguska (Drowning Bear) while tracking a bear. However, it is hard to imagine that Native Americans did not know about the existence of Alum Cave hundreds, if not thousands, of years ago. European settlers visited the site early in the 1800s. In the 1830s a group of men from the Oconaluftee area on the North Carolina side of the Smokies formed the Epsom Salts Manufacturing Co. and began mining Epsom salts, a popular cure-all at the time. Little is known about this mining, but property records indicate that at least some mining continued at the site until the late 1800s. Contrary to popular opinion, Col. William Holland Thomas and his Confederate soldiers did not mine saltpeter at the cave during the Civil War.

As recreational hiking became more popular in the 1920s, and promotion grew for the Smokies as a potential site for a national park, the hike to Alum Cave became a classic visitor experience. Alum Cave first comes into view for the hiker as they round a bend in the trail at Inspiration Point, not far after a set of stone steps takes them through Arch Rock. The most iconic view of Alum Cave, however is from the upper end of the cave itself, an image captured in many a photograph.

Extending to the south of Alum Cave is the knife-edged crest of Duckhawk Ridge. Look for the hole in the ridge known as the "Eye of the Needle." The fortunate hiker may also spot a pair of Peregrine falcons who nest in the area, a reminder that Alum Cave is part of Peregrine Peak and Duckhawk is a common colloquial term for the species. Duckhawk Ridge has been closed to hikers by the NPS due to safety concerns and to protect falcon nesting sites.

Photos by Joel Anderson

Look for the
PEREGRINE FALCON

<ALUM CAVE 18" x 24" Poster art created in 2017 by Michael Korfhage & Joel Anderson

LeConte Lodge

Great Smoky Mountains National Park Archives

A MEMORABLE WAY to experience the awesome beauty and quietude of Mount Le Conte is to spend the night at LeConte Lodge. Accessible only by hiking trails measuring from 5.5 to 8.2 miles in length, it is the highest guest lodge in the eastern United States at 6,360 feet. The site contains seven rustic cabins, three multi-room lodges, a dining hall, and a recreation building. It can accommodate 60 guests.

The site began hosting overnight visitors in July 1925 when the Great Smoky Mountains Conservation Association (a group in Knoxville, Tennessee promoting the creation of Great Smoky Mountains National Park) hired Paul Adams, accompanied by his faithful German shepherd Smoky Jack, to build some rough shelters to provide accommodations for hikers coming to

the summit. Adams hosted the site, staying over the winter, until he was replaced in May 1926 by Jack Huff whose family owned and operated the Mountain View Hotel in Gatlinburg. Huff built the first lodge at the site that summer and with his wife Pauline operated it for 35 years.

Huff's mother heard about the wonderful views from Le Conte and desperately wanted to see them for herself. However, she feared she would be physically unable to make the long, steep climb. In the summer of 1928, Jack, being an obliging son, took a ladder-back chair, attached leather straps so he could wear it like a backpack, and carried his mother up the mountain in style.

Visitors today can retrace the steps of Paul Adams, Smoky Jack, and Jack Huff (and Park Service rules do not

preclude someone from carrying their mother to the top) and stay overnight in the lodge. The accommodations are primitive with no electricity and no running water in the cabins. Visitors are provided with a kerosene lantern, a propane heater, and a wash basin. A bathhouse does have running water and flush toilets, but no showers. The price of a night's stay includes a hot dinner (welcome after the long climb up the mountain) and breakfast. Supplies for the site are brought in by helicopter before the season starts and fresh foods are brought in by llama train along the Trillium Gap Trail.

Reservations are required and the site, managed by a concessionaire, is open from March to November.

LECONTE LODGE 18" x 24" Poster art created in 2017 by Derek Anderson & Joel Anderson >

Smoky Jack

Paul J. Adams Photograph Collection,
University of Tennessee, Knoxville Libraries

ONE INCREDIBLE STORY of the Great Smoky Mountains and Mount Le Conte is the true tale of Smoky Jack. Jack was the faithful 90-pound German Shepherd companion of Paul Adams, the first caretaker of the site that became LeConte Lodge. When Adams was hired in 1925 by the Great Smoky Mountains Conservation Association, he decided to purchase a dog to serve as company and protection as there were plenty of bears and still a few gray wolves in the Smokies.

Jack was originally owned by a police detective in Knoxville (he was known then as Cumberland Jack) and had developed a local reputation for aiding in the capture of several criminals. When the detective was killed in a shoot-out, his widow decided to sell the dog. After meeting Adams, she liked both him and his reasons for wanting a dog. She sold Jack to him at a discount and agreed to let the young man pay her over time.

Smoky Jack proved to be the ideal companion and protector for Adams as he stayed on Le Conte from July 1925 to May 1926. In true Lassie and Rin Tin Tin fashion, Jack tracked and aided in the rescue of several lost hikers and even helped Adams back to camp when he fell from a ridge in Huggins Hell, one of the most rugged and remote sections of the Smokies. According to Adams, the only time Jack showed any fear was when he once encountered a lone wolf.

In addition to these exploits, Smoky Jack earned the most fame for his solo trips to Ogle's Store in Gatlinburg where he picked up mail and supplies for his master. Adams had a custom pack saddle made for Jack from a Calvary officer's briefcase and map case, enabling the big German Shepherd to carry up to 30 pounds of goods up the mountain. Visitors to Le Conte were often startled to see Jack heading down the mountain alone with his saddle bags and coming back up fully laden.

It should be noted here that while dogs are allowed in the Park, they are not allowed on most Park trails or in the backcountry. You can read more about Smoky Jack in *Smoky Jack: The Adventures of a Dog and His Master on Mount Le Conte* written by Paul J. Adams and published by the University of Tennessee Press in 2016.

Courtesy of Tennessee State Library and Archives

Paul Adams and his loyal dog Smoky Jack

Gatlinburg, TN
Charlie Ogle's Store

—Present-day Park Boundary

Round-trip Distance: 20.4 miles

N

—Cherokee Orchard Rd.

Rainbow Falls Trail—

Mount Le Conte
—**Clifftop Campsite**

Courtesy of Tennessee State Library and Archives

<SMOKY JACK Poster art based on a 27" x 36" oil painting created in 2017 by Kai Carpenter

Chimney Tops

Photos by Open Parks Network

THE STEEP TREK to Chimney Tops is one of the most popular hiking destinations in the Smokies. The 1.9 mile Chimney Tops trail climbs along the scenic stream beds of Road Prong and Walker Prong, through cove hardwood forest, and climbs 1,400 feet culminating in two bare outcrops of Anakeesta slate "chimneys" which offer spectacular views of the Sugarlands Mountain, Mount Kephart, and Mount Le Conte.

The trailhead is at a parking area along Newfound Gap Road. The trail begins with a bridge over the Road Prong, a great place for wading and rock hopping. It then begins to gradually climb through old-growth hemlocks, tuliptrees, and beeches and crosses Walker Prong on another bridge. One old Fraser magnolia near the end of this bridge has eight trunks. At about one mile, the trail intersects Road Prong Trail, a vestige of the ancient Indian Gap Trail. Above this intersection the trail

passes through a section of impressive old-growth yellow buckeye trees. Mountain tradition has it that carrying a buckeye in one's pocket will bring good luck.

At this point the trail begins its steepest climb, gaining almost 1,000 feet in the last mile. Up until recent years much of the trail was badly eroded, with exposed rocks and roots, and lots of mud. Beginning in 2012, the trail was completely redone in a herculean effort by the Park Service's "Trails Forever" crew, a group funded by a multi-million dollar endowment created by the Friends of the Smokies. The rehabilitated trail is now characterized by a series of stone stairways composed of 367 individual steps each weighing over 300 pounds.

The trail tops out at an exposed two-humped outcropping of black slate, part of the Anakeesta bedrock formation that runs through the heart of the park. For generations, hikers have enjoyed

scrambling over the rocks and the spectacular views from the top. However, as a result of the Gatlinburg - Chimney Tops Fire in November 2016 (which began near the peaks), vegetation at the top was severely damaged. The resulting erosion has created an extremely unstable and unsafe situation; the trail to the top has partially slid down the mountain. For the time being, the Park Service has closed access to the rock face, and the trail tops out at a vantage point just below the peaks. Visitors should heed Park Service directions and stay off the peaks in order to avoid injury.

Despite the limitations imposed by the 2016 fire damage, hiking Chimney Tops Trail remains one of the top experiences in the Smokies. The hike, however, is not for the faint of heart or those with health issues. Appropriately sturdy footwear is a must for hiking to Chimney Tops; this is definitely not a trail for high heels or flip-flops.

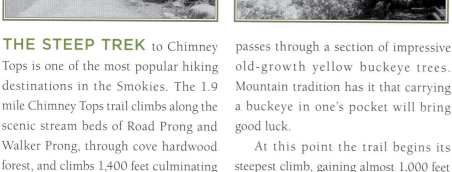

EXTRAS

HIKING HINT:
The best time to visit Chimney Tops is on weekdays during the spring or fall. This trail is so popular during the summertime, it can be nearly impossible to find a parking spot at the trailhead.

DID YOU KNOW?
A southern Appalachian staple, Fraser magnolia trees produce creamy white, pie-sized blossoms in the springtime.

Look for the
FLYING SQUIRREL

<CHIMNEY TOPS 18" x 24" Poster art created in 2017 by Aaron Johnson & Joel Anderson

GREAT SMOKY
MOUNTAINS
NATIONAL PARK

CHARLIES BUNION

Charlies Bunion

Great Smoky Mountains National Park Archives

CHARLIES BUNION provides one of the most spectacular views along the entire 2,200 mile length of the Appalachian Trail. Like Chimney Tops and Alum Cave, it is an exposure of the black slate that composes the Anakeesta Formation, the bedrock of much of the Great Smoky Mountains. Unlike its sister formations, however, Charlies Bunion was not the result of totally natural forces. In fact, human activity played a key role in its creation.

The Bunion came into being as the result of a convergence of calamities. In 1925, a massive wildfire swept up the mountain from Kephart Prong, fueled by slash (dried out branches and small trees) left behind when Champion Fibre Co. clear-cut the hardwood forest. The fire, which consumed over 400 acres, raced up the ridge and burned so intensely at the ridgetop that it mineralized the soil, preventing regrowth. In 1927, a massive thunderstorm hit the area and washed the top soil off the ridge,

exposing the rock that became known as Charlies Bunion. Knoxville lawyer Harvey Broome, one of the founders of the Wilderness Society, asserted, Charlies Bunion serves as "a barren monument to man's carelessness with fire and nature's excess with water."

Originally known by local settlers as Fodderstack, this peculiar cairn got its name as a result of an expedition to the site that included noted Smokies author Horace Kephart, Japanese photographer George Masa (who produced many iconic photographs of the Smokies in the 1920s and 30s), and local mountaineer Charlie Conner who lived in the Oconaluftee area of the Smokies. A variety of stories have been recorded about the conversations that resulted in the naming of the peak. The gist of it is that Conner complained about his foot hurting on the way up the ridge (it's up for debate as to whether he actually had a bunion or not). When

the party got to the newly exposed rock, Kephart joked that it looked like "Charlie's bunion." It so happened that Kephart and Masa were on the North Carolina Nomenclature Commission charged with naming untitled peaks, creeks, and other geographical features, so the moniker has stuck memorializing Charlie's sore foot to this day.

While Broome called the Bunion a "barren monument," the site attracts throngs of hikers in the summer and on weekends. It is a gorgeous hike along the main ridge of the Smokies over Mount Ambler and down to the rocks. The views of Mount Le Conte, Mount Kephart, the Jump Off, and Mount Guyot on a clear day well reward the effort of the relatively strenuous 8-mile roundtrip trek. The view into the Greenbrier section of the Park is especially stunning as the terrain drops over 2,000 feet down into the drainage of the East Fork of the Little Pigeon River. That drop is one reason to exercise caution at the site and especially to keep a close eye on the children.

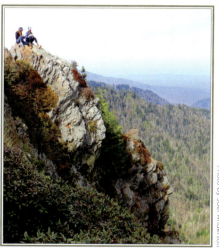

Photo by Joel Anderson

<CHARLIES BUNION 18" x 24" Poster art created in 2017 by Michael Korfhage & Joel Anderson

GREAT SMOKY
MOUNTAINS
— NATIONAL PARK —

APPALACHIAN TRAIL

Appalachian Trail

Members of the Smoky Mountain Hiking Club "Vacation Hikers" in 1933

THE WORLD-FAMOUS

Appalachian Trail (the "AT") stretches approximately 2,200 miles from Springer Mountain, Georgia to the top of Mount Katahdin, Maine. Seventy-one of its most scenic, and most hiked, miles run through the heart of Great Smoky Mountains National Park. The Smokies also contain the longest continuous stretch of trail above 5,000 feet from Silers Bald to Cosby Knob.

Hiking the AT through the Smokies takes the visitor through vastly different worlds. Beginning at Fontana Dam, the first half of the trail climbs almost 5,000 feet to Clingmans Dome, the highest spot on the entire trail, before rolling down about 4,500 feet to Davenport Gap. Along the way, the hiker experiences wide vistas from peaks and mountain balds such as Shuckstack, Spence Field, Thunderhead Mountain, Silers Bald, Clingmans Dome, Newfound Gap, Charlies Bunion, Mount Guyot, and Mount Cammerer. The trail also takes hikers through a variety of ecosystems: thick cove hardwood forests; pine-clad south-facing ridges; heath balds covered in rhododendron, mountain laurel, and flame azalea which bloom spectacularly in June; grass balds once used to graze thousands of cattle in the summers; and high elevation spruce/fir forests more akin to ecosystems in Canada than to the Southern Appalachians.

The Appalachian Trail began as a vision of regional planner Benton MacKaye who first proposed the idea in 1921. Myron Avery, and several others, helped organize hiking clubs in areas near the trail to make it a reality. Although the path has been changed and adapted over the years, the original routing, clearing, and blazing of the trail through the Smokies was done by the Smoky Mountains Hiking Club of Knoxville, Tennessee. They still help maintain it today. In 1968, the Trail, with the quiet support of Lady Bird Johnson, became the first National Scenic Trail under the management of the National Park Service. NPS manages and protects the trail in cooperation with the Appalachian Trail Conservancy, a non-profit organization based near the mid-point of the AT in Harper's Ferry, West Virginia. The last major stretch of the AT that passed through private lands was acquired by the federal government in 2014.

While most visitors to the Smokies take a short out-and-back hike on the AT from Newfound Gap, Fontana Dam, or the parallel Clingmans Dome Road, backpacking the AT allows those willing to brave its rocky tread and steep climbs to witness some of the most remote, and most beautiful, areas of the Park. Backpackers are not allowed to camp along the trail and must use one of 12 shelters scattered along the way. Shelter reservations can be made at the GSMNP website.

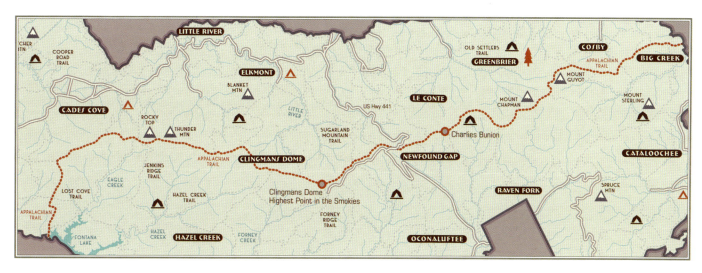

<APPALACHIAN TRAIL Poster art based on a 27" x 36" oil painting created in 2017 by Kai Carpenter

Highest Point in the Smokies

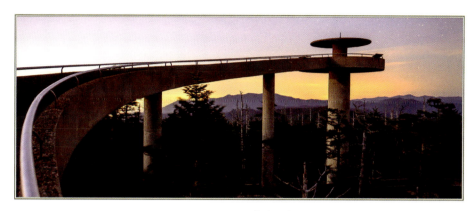

AT 6,643 FEET, Clingmans Dome is the highest point in the Smokies, the highest in Tennessee, the highest on the Appalachian Trail, and the third highest peak in eastern North America. It is crowned with a distinctive observation tower which provides 360° views of the Smokies and adjacent mountains. Clingmans Dome Road brings visitors from Newfound Gap to within one-half mile of the summit where they can hike to the peak along a steep but paved trail.

The drive up Clingmans Dome Road is the best opportunity in the Park for visitors to view a high elevation Southern Appalachian spruce-fir forest from their automobiles. Such forests are a rare ecosystem that exist only above 5,500 feet in elevation and are dominated by two types of evergreen trees: the red spruce and the Fraser fir. These highland forests harbor a number of animal species rare to the region including the spruce-fir moss spider, the northern flying squirrel, the pygmy salamander, Blackburnian warblers, and northern saw-whet owls.

Visitors will quickly note the presence of the ghostly white trunks of thousands of dead Fraser firs all along Clingmans Dome Road and on the summit of the mountain. This massive die-off is the result of an infestation by the balsam wooly adelgid, a tiny wingless insect which first came to the Smokies around 1957. The adelgid has killed more than 90% of the mature firs in the area. The Fraser fir die-off has also affected the red spruce which are now more exposed to the high winds characteristic of this elevation. Some scientists argue that damage from the adelgid is more severe than it ordinarily would have been due to the weakening of the trees' immune systems as a result of acid rain and ozone pollution.

Unfortunately, plagues affecting a tree species are a fact of modern life in the Great Smoky Mountains National Park. The chestnut blight wiped out the American chestnut (once the most common tree in the Smokies) in the 1920s, '30s and '40s, and the hemlock wooly adelgid hit the Park in 2002 and has killed almost 80% of the eastern hemlocks, including some massive trees in old-growth forests. In recent years, other invasives have attacked and decimated dogwoods, butternuts, and mountain ash. In an effort to keep these damaging invasive insects out of the Park, the NPS now requires campers to use specially treated firewood in campgrounds and picnic areas.

Despite the damage to the Fraser firs, Clingmans Dome is still a magical place. The Cherokee traditionally considered it a sacred site known as Kuwa' hi, or mulberry place, home to the great White Bear, chief of all the bears. Today the allure of its dramatic views attracts scores of visitors, including many couples making marriage proposals.

The 7-mile Clingmans Dome Road is open from April 1 to November 30. It ends in a large parking lot, which can fill early in summer and fall, half-a-mile from the summit. The road also provides access to the Smokies backcountry along the Appalachian Trail, Forney Ridge Trail (which leads to Andrews Bald, one of the most accessible mountain balds in the Smokies), Road Prong Trail, Sugarlands Mountain Trail, Noland Divide Trail, and Forney Creek Trail.

Photo by Brian Schrayer

"Away out yonder beyond the mighty bulk of Clingman Dome, which, black with spruce and balsam, looked like a vast bear rising to contemplate the northern world, there streaked the first faint, nebulous hint of dawn. Presently the big bear's head was tipped with a golden crown flashing against the scarlet fires of the firmament, and the earth awoke." — Horace Kephart: *Our Southern Highlanders*, 1913

<CLINGMANS DOME Poster art based on a 30" x 40" acrylic painting created in 2017 by Joel Anderson

Cherokee

NO ONE REALLY KNOWS exactly when the Cherokee, the Ani-Yun-Wiya in their language, first came to the Great Smoky Mountains. But for much of the past 1,000 years they have been the primary human inhabitants of the area. As such, they have both shaped and been shaped by these mountains in dramatic ways. While the Cherokee inhabited much of North Georgia, Northeast Alabama, East Tennessee, Upstate South Carolina, and Western North Carolina, they consider the Smokies as the center of their homeland, and Kituah (a mound site near the southern border of the Park between Cherokee and Bryson City) as their "Mother Town."

The Cherokee were not a united political entity until the 1800s and, prior to the coming of Europeans, lived in independent villages and towns located in river and stream bottoms near the most arable land. They were, however, united by language, one closely related to the Iroquoian languages of the tribes of western Pennsylvania and New York, indicating possible migration from that area. Their culture and social organization also united them, most importantly their system of seven clans.

Cherokee life revolved around the clans and the roughly translated names are the "Wild Potato," "Long Hair," "Deer," "Blue," "Bird," "Wolf," and "Paint." Membership in the clans was determined at birth and, as the Cherokee were traditionally a matrilineal society, one was automatically in the clan of one's mother. Certain roles were often accorded to individuals based on their clan membership, for instance members of the Bird Clan were known as messengers, Paint Clan members for their medical skills, and Wolves as protectors. Village members sat by clan in the council house under distinctive symbols.

Marriage to a fellow clan member was strictly forbidden and clan members were required to seek retribution from those who hurt or killed their kin.

A lifestyle based on agriculture, gathering, and hunting also unified the Cherokee. Cherokee agriculture focused on the sacred "Three Sisters;" corn, beans, and a variety of squash-related plants including pumpkins, gourds, and water-

Cherokee Dance Mask

melons. Women conducted most of the agriculture and were considered the owners of the fields. The Cherokee also spent part of the year away from the village at temporary camp sites where they gathered nuts, berries, and medicinal herbs. Men hunted a variety of animals including turkeys, groundhogs, squirrels, and rabbits using blowguns and bows year round and went on long late fall and early winter hunts as far away as Kentucky in search of larger game such as deer and bear and on occasions elk or buffalo. Men were also warriors and spent part of their year seeking out enemy tribes, particularly in areas that were claimed as prime hunting grounds by several tribes.

Fire, also seen as a sacred force, gave the Cherokee the ability to manage the environment of the Smokies to support their favored subsistence activities. They burned the ground around their villages to better spot approaching enemies and keep insects and snakes away. They burned their fields to clear them of trees and brush, and after each harvest to clear away old growth and replenish the soil. They managed the mountain forests by lighting low-intensity fires to keep the forest clear of undergrowth and make enemies or game easier to spot. It also stimulated growth of plant shoots which attracted deer and turkeys and facilitated easier travel. Because sites like Gregory Bald are mentioned in traditional Cherokee folk tales, some scholars believe they used fire to maintain naturally formed mountain balds as attractors for deer.

Over the centuries, the Cherokee developed a rich ceremonial life with a variety of festivals and celebrations. The most important of these was the Green Corn Ceremony which came in late summer when the crops were ripening and needed little tending. This was a time for renewal, the re-kindling of hearth fires from the sacred fire which burned in the council house, a time of marriage and of divorce, and a time of feasting and dancing. One of the most anticipated events of any festival among the Cherokee was the ball game, an early relative of lacrosse played by men with two sticks instead of one. As anthropologist James Mooney described the game among the Cherokee in the 1890s, equal-sized teams square off on the field with the goal to carry a deer-hide ball across the opposing team's end zone. In the process, as Mooney described it, "almost anything short of murder is allowable." The Cherokee called the game the "little brother of war." The first team to score twelve goals wins and games could last all day.

<CHEROKEE WOMAN Poster art based on a 27" x 36" oil painting created in 2017 by Kai Carpenter

Examples of Cherokee basket weaving

Contact with Europeans from the 1500s to the 1800s disrupted this rich and complex lifestyle. Most significantly, the introduction of communicable diseases to which the Cherokee had no immunity (such as smallpox, mumps, and measles) decimated the tribe. Major epidemics struck in 1698, 1738-39, and 1759-60, reducing tribal numbers by as much as three-fourths. The Cherokee also became more and more tied to European commercial activities as demand for deer, elk, beaver, and otter hides and furs skyrocketed and the Cherokee became major suppliers to Charleston and Savannah traders. The Cherokee became increasingly dependent on trade goods, and the fur craze made hunting for their own food much more difficult.

The Cherokee also suffered when they became embroiled in European wars. They well understood their self interest, but unfortunately, the countries they backed invariably lost. In the French and Indian War they backed the French and suffered from British retribution. In the American Revolution, they backed the British and lost substantial territory and hundreds of tribe members in battles with the newly formed United States of America.

By the late 1700s and early 1800s, many

Cherokee had decided that their only way to survive as a people was to emulate the lifestyle of European settlers and become a "civilized" tribe. Many Cherokee adopted European farming methods, particularly livestock husbandry, and abandoned the long hunt. The Cherokee also formed

> "An old Cherokee told his Grandson: 'My Son, there is a battle between two wolves inside us all. One is Evil; it is anger, jealousy, greed, resentment, inferiority, lies and ego. The other is Good; it is joy, peace, love, hope, humility, kindness and truth.' He thought about it and asked, 'Grandfather, which wolf wins?' The Grandfather replied: 'The one you feed.'"
> — *Cherokee proverb*

a centralized government patterned after the U.S. Constitution; adopted a written syllabary invented by a Cherokee named Sequoyah; built schools for their children; established The Cherokee One Feather, a tribal newspaper; some converted to Christianity.

Ultimately, however, the "civilization"

program was unsuccessful and pressure increased on the U.S. government, particularly with the election of Andrew Jackson and the rise of the Democratic Party, to move the Cherokee west to what was then called "Indian Territory" (modern day Oklahoma). Although the Cherokee resisted this with all their might and resources, including two successful appeals to the U.S. Supreme Court which the Jackson administration ignored, they were forced to move. A group of unauthorized Cherokee fraudulently negotiated the Treaty of New Echota with the U.S. government and ceded all Cherokee tribal land in exchange for an equal amount of land in Indian Territory, plus $5,000,000 and money to cover the expenses of the move.

In 1838, the U.S. Army under Gen. Winfield Scott began rounding up the Cherokee, placing them in "forts" under horrible conditions before moving them west over the so-called "Trail of Tears." Thousands of Cherokee died (estimates range from 4,000 to 10,000) as a result of abusive conditions on the trail and the physical and mental stress of a 2,200 mile journey during the bitter winter months.

An obvious question that arises when individuals come to Great Smoky Mountains National Park is, given this history, how are there still Cherokee in the Smokies? The answer is long and complex, but a short answer is that the ancestors of the current members of the Eastern Band of Cherokee Indians were able to take advantage of a legal loophole. While Cherokee lore attributes the Eastern Band's escape to the sacrificial act of a Cherokee named Tsali (a story told in the outdoor drama "Unto These Hills"), the reality is that most of the Cherokee who remained were not living on tribal land. Most of them lived on land near Quallatown, a settlement owned by William Holland Thomas, the adopted son of a local chief named Yonaguska or "Drowning Bear."

Cherokee women making pottery

A wealthy merchant and lawyer, Thomas skillfully negotiated the political waters of Washington, D.C. and the state capital in Raleigh to enable the Quallatown Cherokee, and a few scattered groups from the far western tip of the state, to remain in their Smokies homeland. Cherokee who had hid out in the mountains until the soldiers left and some who made the long trek back from Indian Territory joined later. All told, about 1,200 Cherokee were able to stay, though it should be noted that their land was remote and poor. As historian John Finger observed, "it is apparent that they exist only in those areas considered unattractive by whites during the nineteenth century."

In the years after removal, the Eastern Band lived a rather precarious existence. They fought ongoing efforts to remove them and remained trapped in legal limbo with both the state and federal government. In 1866, the State of North Carolina officially recognized the right of the Cherokee to stay. This was primarily in recognition of the tribal members who, under the leadership of William Holland Thomas, served in the Confederate Army. In 1868, Washington officially recognized the Eastern Band as separate from the Cherokee west of the Mississippi. The group's lands (now called the Qualla Boundary) were put in a trust under the stewardship of the federal government in 1924.

In the late 1800s and early years of the 20th century, the Cherokee of the Smokies scratched out a meager existence on hardscrabble farms. Many tribe members maintained their native language and traditional ways, especially in more isolated areas like Big Cove and Snowbird. In the early years of the 20th century, life began to change for the Eastern Band. As more middle class Americans bought cars and the Great Smoky Mountains grew more popular, the town of Cherokee became a booming tourist destination, especially when it became the primary North Carolina gateway to the Park in the 1930s.

During the 1930s, 40s, and 50s Cherokee souvenir shops, restaurants, motels, and tourist cabins proliferated. However, the image sold to tourists was not authentically Cherokee and was more reflective of the dress and dances

Cherokee man "Chiefing"

of western tribes like the Sioux and Hopi. Over the years, some Cherokee made a living doing what was called "chiefing," standing next to the highway in a big feathered headdress and buckskins posing for pictures with tourists.

In the late 1940s a concern among tribal

members that authentic Cherokee culture and history were not being preserved led to the creation of the Museum of the Cherokee Indian and the Cherokee Historical Association. The Museum opened in 1948 and now houses the largest and most complete collection of Cherokee artifacts in the world. CHA commissioned the creation of the outdoor drama "Unto These Hills" and created the adjacent outdoor Cherokee life and culture museum, the Oconaluftee Indian Village. Both continue to operate in the warmer months to this day.

Despite the tourist boom, most of the Cherokee of the Smokies region lived a very modest life, farming, commuting to industrial jobs in nearby towns, or working in seasonal tourism jobs. The seasonality and general uncertainties of life caused many young people to leave the Qualla Boundary and try to make their fortunes elsewhere.

In 1997, the tribe's prospects changed dramatically when Harrah's Cherokee Casino opened on the eastern side of Cherokee. Because the lands of the Eastern Band are in a federal trust, the tribe is exempt from state law, including laws banning casino gambling. The ever-expanding casino operations attract tens of thousands of visitors each year and bring millions of dollars to the tribe and enrolled tribe members who receive annual payouts from casino profits. The tribe has used casino revenues to improve healthcare and education (Cherokee has a state-of-the-art K-12 school that includes a facsimile council house divided into seven sections, one for each Cherokee clan), as well as to preserve and teach the Cherokee language, and maintain and improve the tribe's cultural and historic sites.

In a highly significant and symbolic move, in 1996, the tribe purchased the site of Kituah from the white family that had farmed it for generations. Now the site of their "Mother Town" is back in the hands of the Cherokee.

Mountain Farm Museum

EUROPEAN SETTLERS established themselves in the Great Smoky Mountains as the Cherokee were gradually pushed back in the early 19th century. They settled primarily in river and creek bottoms, often on Cherokee "old fields," and lived a lifestyle based on the "three sisters" similar to those they displaced. Early settlers also formed trading networks in livestock, hides and furs, medicinal herbs (most notably ginseng), and whiskey.

The Park commemorates the lifestyle of 19th century Smokies pioneers with preserved log cabins, barns, water-powered mills, and out-buildings scattered throughout the Park. The most notable sites are at the Mountain Farm Museum near the Oconaluftee Visitor Center, in Cades Cove, and along the Roaring Fork Motor Nature Road. The Mountain Farm Museum shows visitors how a working farm looked during the 19th century with its cabin made of hewn chestnut logs, apple house, meat house, chicken house, corn cribs, blacksmith shop, and spring house. The buildings were moved to the site in the early 1950s

(the large barn came in 1960) and the Museum opened for visitors in 1953. The site also contains live hogs and chickens, fenced fields where corn and other typical pioneer crops are cultivated, and a small apple orchard featuring heirloom apple varieties.

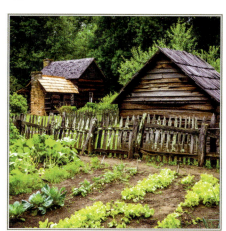

Gardens at the Mountain Farm Museum

Although the NPS tries to keep the site historically accurate, visitors will note the elaborate split-rail fencing of the garden and the wire fencing around the apple trees. The fences protect the crops from ravenous elk who would wipe out the crops if allowed. Of course, the early settlers had a solution to this

problem not available to the Park Service: they could shoot and eat them.

The Mountain Farm Museum hosts a number of events each year where visitors can see live demonstrations of such activities as soap making and turning raw sorghum into molasses. The Women's Work Festival is held in June and highlights the many roles women played on mountain farms. In September, the site hosts the Mountain Life Festival with music and dancing as well as demonstrations of traditional activities. NPS staff also organize periodic Back Porch Old-Time Music Jams on the porch of the Oconaluftee Visitor Center on Saturday afternoons. Visitors can either sit back and enjoy the music or bring their own instruments and join a Smoky Mountains jam session.

Half-a-mile north of the Mountain Farm Museum, visitors can also see how the pioneers ground their corn at the historic Mingus Mill. A mill was first built at this site in 1886 and the current one was reconstructed by the CCC in 1937. The mill is open daily from mid-March to mid-November.

<PIONEER WOMAN Poster art based on a 27" x 36" oil painting created in 2017 by Kai Carpenter

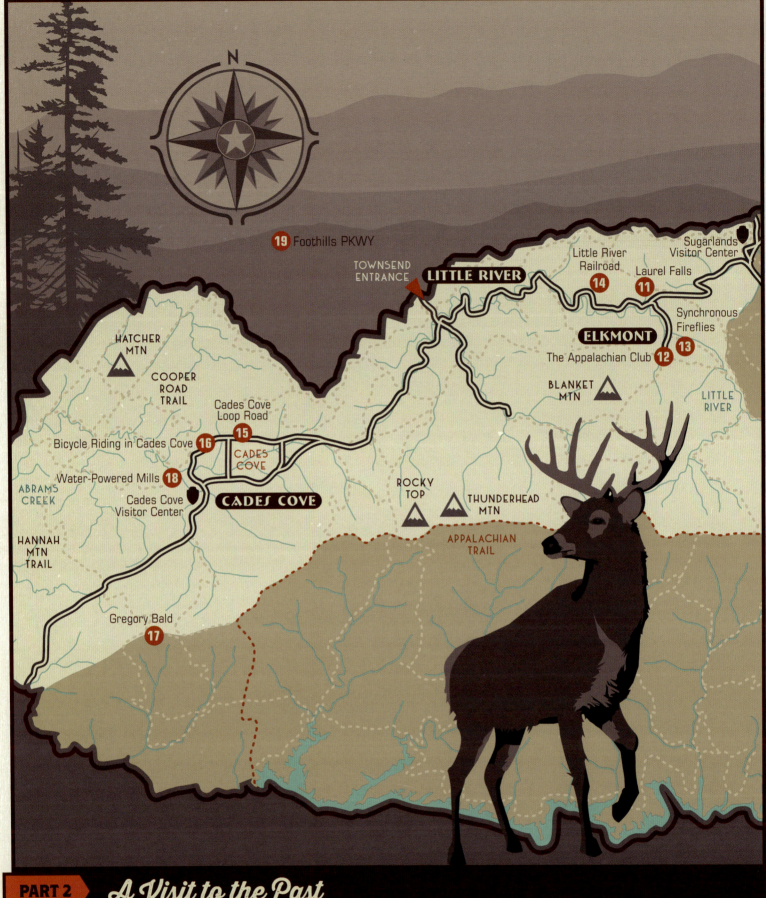

N

19 Foothills PKWY

TOWNSEND
ENTRANCE

LITTLE RIVER

Little River
Railroad

Sugarlands
Visitor Center

14 Laurel Falls

11

Synchronous
Fireflies

ELKMONT

HATCHER
MTN

COOPER
ROAD
TRAIL

The Appalachian Club 12   13

BLANKET
MTN

LITTLE
RIVER

Cades Cove
Loop Road

Bicycle Riding in Cades Cove 16   15

CADES
COVE

ROCKY
TOP

THUNDERHEAD
MTN

Water-Powered Mills 18

ABRAMS
CREEK

Cades Cove
Visitor Center

CADES COVE

APPALACHIAN
TRAIL

HANNAH
MTN
TRAIL

Gregory Bald

17

PART 2   *A Visit to the Past*

A Visit to the Past

The Northwest Section of the Park (Sugarlands to Cades Cove)

Photo by Joel Anderson

Little River Road stretches from its junction with Newfound Gap Road to a fork in the Little River called the Townsend Y. From here, Laurel Creek Road runs all the way to Cades Cove. This northwest section of the Park, though filled with remarkable scenery, is recognized as a gateway into the Smoky Mountain's rich human history.

In a world surrounded by mountains, Cades Cove is startlingly flat. Preserved cabins, barns, churches, and water-powered mills offer a glimpse into the lives of the Park's early European settlers on this broad plain. The buildings and graveyards also serve as testimony to the sacrifice of over 4,000 inhabitants who were forcibly removed in the 1920s-30s to make way for a national park. From a recreational standpoint, the Cades Cove Loop is an excellent place for a bike ride. Due to its gorgeous setting, this 11-mile drive is a popular summertime destination for cyclists who enjoy car-free roads until

10 a.m. twice a week (May-September, Wednesday and Saturday mornings).

Ambling along a beautiful mountain stream, Little River Road follows a railroad grade cut by the Little River Railroad and Lumber Company in the

John Oliver Cabin, Cades Cove

Photo by Brian Schrayer

early years of the 20th century. This railroad stretched from Townsend to Elkmont, bringing thousands of workers, steam logging equipment, and a new way of life for the people of the region. It also carried away billions of board feet of prime hardwood timber. Now that timber cutting has ceased, the Little River is a cheerful spot to

stop and explore. Numerous stream beds make for prime rock hopping while the paved trail to 80-foot Laurel Falls is a moderate one-mile hike from the parking area.

Nature seems to have reclaimed the Elkmont region for its own, especially in the Appalachian Club area. Back in the early 1900s, Knoxville's elite began building summer homes at Elkmont. Though this neighborhood became federal property in the 1930s, many of the cottage owners sold their land in exchange for 20-year leases (which were quietly renegotiated and extended until even the early 1990s). Some of these now-empty homes are preserved by the Park. If you happen to visit Elkmont in late spring, you might witness one of the Park's most dazzling natural spectacles. Thanks to the synchronous firefly, Nature needs no electricity to light up the night sky. The NPS hosts an annual firefly festival here in late May, early June.

Laurel Falls

Open Parks Network

LAUREL FALLS is perhaps the most popular waterfall in the Park due to its relative ease of access. The 80-foot tall cascade can be reached via the paved Laurel Falls Trail which begins in a parking area at Fighting Creek Gap along Little River Road. The trail crosses a picturesque wooden bridge that bisects the falls and enables visitors to get to the other side of Laurel Branch with dry feet.

A 1.3-mile walk on a paved trail leads visitors to the falls. The trail was first built in 1935 by CCC crews who had to blast through rock to create a pathway that hugs the mountainside. In the 1960s, the NPS paved the trail. While the Park Service has improved accessibility, Laurel Falls Trail still has its challenges. It is fairly steep in spots and gains over 300 feet in total incline, hindering wheelchair access. The section of trail approaching the falls also has steep drop-offs down into the gorge of Laurel Creek (what locals call the "Devil's Chute," for understandable reasons) and visitors with children need to keep an eye on them here.

The falls themselves are a delight to the eyes and ears and they provide a cool respite on hot days. They can, however, be crowded and it can be difficult to find a parking space during peak seasons and on weekends. For the best light for pictures, go early in the morning or late afternoon. These are also the best times to enjoy the sound of the falls and the play of sunlight on the water in solitude. Laurel Falls puts on a particularly spectacular show during high water or when they freeze during extreme winter cold snaps.

For those with the energy and inclination, Laurel Falls Trail continues past the falls for three miles through old-growth forests and on to the top of Cove Mountain, a peak with great views of the surrounding highlands. The trail is much less crowded here and much quieter as you pass through a section of huge tuliptrees, buckeyes, basswoods, and Fraser magnolias. The trail intersects Cove Mountain Trail after four miles and hikers can make the short trip to the top of Cove Mountain to enjoy the views. Cove Mountain is crowned with an old firetower, but visitor access to the mountaintop is blocked by an air quality monitoring station.

Laurel Falls is popular for a number of reasons, but visitors should keep in mind the dangers waterfalls can pose. Every year people are seriously injured, and even die, as a result of trying to climb on the slick rocks of area waterfalls. The Park Service urges visitors to enjoy sites like Laurel Falls from the safety of the trail.

LAUREL FALLS 18" x 24" Poster art created in 2017 by Derek Anderson and Joel Anderson >

Great
SMOKY MOUNTAINS
NATIONAL PARK

LAUREL FALLS

The Appalachian Club

IN 2014 the Huffington Post published a blog post entitled "Hiker Discovers an Abandoned Town Inside Great Smoky Mountains National Park." The post soon went viral on social media and people all over the world were set to wondering about this "ghost town" in the middle of a national park. On closer inspection, however, people with even limited knowledge of the Tennessee side of the Smokies realized that what the writer had "discovered" was not some isolated site in a lost cove, but the abandoned ruins of two once thriving summer home communities. The buildings are actually located on paved roads in the Elkmont section of the Park and right next to the Elkmont Campground, the largest in the Smokies.

While the post was definitely misleading, it did highlight one of the stranger, and more interesting, sites in the Smokies and one worth "discovering" on your own. The "ghost town" the author encountered contains the remains of two resort communities built in the early

1900s and abandoned in the early 1990s. In the early years of the 20th century, the Little River Railroad (originally built as a logging railroad) began running "excursion cars" on weekends to bring visitors up through the scenic gorge of the Little River and to its logging town at Elkmont.

In 1910, Little River Lumber Co. agreed to sell land along Little River to a group of Knoxville elites who formed the Appalachian Club and built a clubhouse and summer homes in what became known as "Daisy Town." Two years later a large resort hotel, the Wonderland Hotel, was built further downstream and in 1919,

members of the rival Wonderland Club bought the hotel and began building summer homes of their own in the area.

The neighborhoods thrived in the 1920s and Tennessee's well-to-do began summering there, including Governor Austin Peay. The future of the communities became uncertain later in the decade, however, as the movement to establish a national park in the Smokies progressed. While small farmers within Park boundaries had their land condemned and were forced to move, the summer home owners in Elkmont were politically well connected. Several of these homeowners played prominent roles in the Park movement, including the most important leader on the Tennessee side, Col. David Chapman. They were able to have their property exempted from the state's power of eminent domain and sold it on favorable terms. In return they received life-time leases which allowed them to continue to use their homes.

The homeowners negotiated twenty-year extensions on their leases in

rapidly deteriorated. Finally, in 2009 the Park Service got all parties to agree to a settlement of the fate of Elkmont's homes and community buildings. They issued its Final Environmental Impact Statement for Elkmont, a plan which called for the restoration of the Appalachian Clubhouse and the Spence Cabin as day-use facilities, and the stabilization of eighteen of Elkmont's oldest and most representative homes in the Daisy Town section. These would stand as a memorial and interpretive site for the summer home experience in the Smokies. In addition, the Byers cabin, which once belonged to the leader of the Smokies National Park movement David Chapman, was added to the list of structures to be stabilized. The rest of the structures in the area were to be carefully documented by Park Service historians and removed.

1950 and 1971; a deal allegedly settled behind closed doors with the Secretary of the Interior by Tennessee U.S. Senator Howard Baker. By the early 1990s, when the leases were once again up for renewal, opposition within the National Park Service and among environmentalists and descendants of the evicted farmers (who had no such opportunity to keep their homes) had grown significantly. Former Smokies farmer Carl Whaley argued, "They got money and some way the government let them live there. We had none. There isn't a thing fair about it." In 1992, the National Park Service announced that the leases would not be renewed and most NPS employees hoped that the area would be cleared of its buildings-many already in poor condition-and returned to wilderness status.

In a last ditch effort to keep their homes, a group of Elkmont residents organized the Elkmont Preservation Committee to seek registration of the homes and buildings on the National Register of Historic Places. While there was no hope that they could use their vacation homes, this did begin a long struggle over what would happen to the buildings between the Park Service, the Tennessee Historical Commission, the National Trust for Historic Preservation, and a new group formed to promote the preservation of the buildings, Friends of Elkmont.

Meanwhile the buildings sat abandoned and decaying. In 2005, the Wonderland Hotel collapsed and the Park Service removed its remains while other structures

The Park Service has begun removal of the more dilapidated dwellings and completed the renovations of the Appalachian Clubhouse and the Spence Cabin (which has a wonderful patio looking out over Little River) and visitors can reserve them for weddings, receptions, and family gatherings. The Daisy Town section still stands in ghostly silence commemorating a by-gone era of the summer home communities located within the Park.

Decaying vacation cottages became safety hazards for Park visitors before they were demolished in 2017

Synchronous Fireflies

Photos by Radim Schreiber / www.fireflyexperience.org

SYNCHRONOUS FIREFLIES (*Photinus carolinus*) are a unique species of firefly found in Great Smoky Mountains National Park, most notably in the Elkmont area. During the mating season the males flash in unison or in waves putting on a spectacular exhibition against the backdrop of the dark forest. The annual display has become so popular with visitors that the National Park Service requires reservations for evening parking at the Sugarlands Visitor Center and transportation via shuttle to the Elkmont area during the peak of synchronous firefly activity. During this period, only those on official shuttle buses or with reservations in the Elkmont Campground are allowed access to the area.

All firefly flashing is part of their mating behavior. The reason for the synchronous display of *Photinus carolinus* is to produce a large amount of light so that the female will recognize the flashing males as members of her own species. Scientists can predict when synchronous flashing will begin by keeping track of daily maximum and minimum air temperatures. Historically, the phenomenon occurs within a two-week period- between late May and early June.

Photinus carolinus, which is one of 19 species of firefly in Great Smoky Mountains National Park, is also found throughout the Southern Appalachians and has been spotted as far north as Pennsylvania. Different species of synchronous fireflies occur in other areas of the world, such as in Southeast Asia, Japan, and in the United States in South Carolina.

The National Park Service advises visitors who want to view the fireflies to cover their flashlights with red cellophane, point them at the ground, and then turn the flashlight off altogether when the firefly flashing begins. In addition, they remind firefly viewers that this is a national park and that all wildlife, including insects, are protected and should not be touched or harmed in any way (nor can they be collected in jars).

The National Park Service announces the dates of the annual "Firefly Event" in late April and those interested in seeing this memorable display can enter the lottery for reservations at that point. The Park Service switched to the lottery system in 2016. In previous years, so many people (up to 15,000 per day) would try to make reservations on the old "first come, first serve" system that they repeatedly crashed the website.

"It's almost an unreal experience to have in nature, it's incredibly special."
— GSMNP Management Assistant, Dana Soehn

SYNCHRONOUS FIREFLIES Poster art based on a 30" x 40" acrylic painting created in 2017 by Joel Anderson >

GREAT SMOKY MOUNTAINS
NATIONAL PARK ⑬ SYNCHRONOUS FIREFLIES

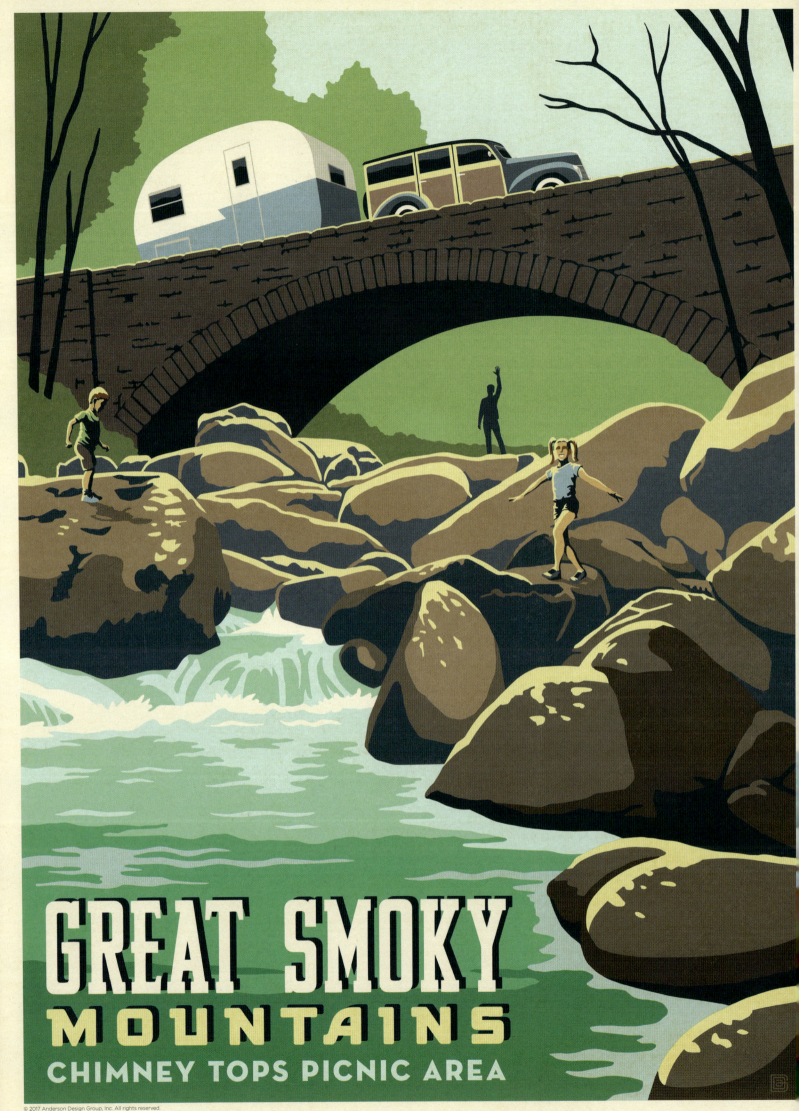

GREAT SMOKY
MOUNTAINS
CHIMNEY TOPS PICNIC AREA

Mountain Streams

FOR MANY VISITORS to Great Smoky Mountains National Park, driving along, hiking beside, or playing in the hundreds of streams that flow out of the mountains provides one of their most memorable experiences. The sights and sounds of the cool, rushing waters amplify the sense of peaceful solitude. For children in particular (who seem to have fewer and fewer opportunities for such activities) the streams of the Smokies provide great opportunities for exploring nature, rock hopping, and splashing in the shallows.

Boulders line and fill most of the Park's streams, enticing many to enjoy the shallows of Little River, the Little Pigeon River, the Oconaluftee River, Big Creek, Cataloochee Creek, Deep Creek, Noland Creek, Hazel Creek and literally hundreds of their tributaries. Children (and adults) willing to get their feet wet, turn over a few rocks, and look closely into a Smokies stream will be well rewarded with a view of a watery world alive with insects, amphibians, and fish. Park giftshops and bookstores operated by the Great Smoky Mountains Association offer books, guides, and fun tools to help children of all ages enjoy and learn from stream exploration.

Visitors should also take advantage of the abundant opportunities to hike away from the crowds, sit on a rock, and enjoy the mystical music of the rushing waters. As author/poet George Ellison, who lives on the edge of the Park, wrote in his book *Permanent Camp*: "Running water is more than a material force . . . it is a spiritual element." Humans have long felt this spiritual draw to the Smokies' creeks and streams. The Cherokee have ancient traditions of "going to water" for spiritual cleansing and renewal. In addition, many pools in the streams (especially in once-settled areas like Sugarlands, Greenbrier, Cades Cove, and Cataloochee) have long histories as sites where churches conducted the sacrament of baptism. For those of a poetic bent like Ellison, a quiet stream setting in the Smokies offers a "place of refuge" and "beckons" people "toward a closer relationship with the natural world."

Visitors should keep in mind that the National Park Service discourages swimming, kayaking, and tubing in Park streams and they need to use extreme caution around water. It is also illegal to move the rocks in a stream to form dams or channels, so if you turn over rocks exploring the creeks and streams, please return them to their original position.

Photos by Joel Anderson

EXTRAS

★ **FUN FACT:**
Gold was discovered in the Little River in the early 1920's. The gold rush didn't last long, however; someone soon realized that for every ton of rocks crushed, only $1.27 of gold could be salvaged.

ⓘ **DID YOU KNOW?**
The Cherokee's traditional name for Cades Cove is "Tsiyahi," the Place of the Otter. Abrams Creek was once a popular swim hole for the Smokies' river otters.

Look for the **STINKPOT TURTLE**

<ROCK HOPPING 18" x 24" Poster art created in 2017 by Aaron Johnson & Joel Anderson

Little River Railroad

FOLKS ARE SURPRISED to learn as they look out over these mountains that in the early years of the 20th century over 400 miles of railroad crisscrossed Great Smoky Mountains National Park and penetrated its deepest recesses. The Little River Railroad was one of the most scenic and storied railroad lines in the Smokies. The railroad linked the lumber mill of the Little River Lumber Company (LRLC) in Townsend, Tennessee with its advanced timber operations in Elkmont eighteen miles away, running along the Little River for much of its length.

Near the turn of the twentieth century, the Pennsylvania-based timber company purchased 80,000 acres of prime hardwood timberland in the Little River watershed. A massive lumber mill was built in the newly created town of Townsend, named after W.B. Townsend, one of LRLC's owners and manager of its Tennessee operations. In 1903, construction began on the railroad line along Little River, gradually progressing upstream as they cut the surrounding timber. In 1908, the rail reached Elkmont. In its almost 40 years of operation, the railroad hauled over 560 million board feet of timber out of the Smokies.

While the route of the railroad is one of the most scenic imaginable, it also had its share of dangers and more than its share of train wrecks. The most famous of these came in 1909 on a rainy afternoon when a train piloted by engineer Gordon "Daddy" Bryson with five heavily loaded log cars went out of control in a steep, curvy section of track near Jakes Creek. According to survivors' accounts, "Daddy" and brakeman Charles Jenkins bravely stayed at their posts battling to keep the train from derailing. Both died in the subsequent accident and survivors hung their dead comrades' empty lunch pails from a nearby tree to commemorate their bravery. Local musicians also memorialized the two with the "Ballad of Daddy Bryson" which soon became a local favorite and is still sung in the area to this day. The plaintive chorus of the ballad goes:

> "How the cinders from the smoke
>   stack were flying
> The brakeman trying
> The train to stop
> Still Daddy stood bravely at his
>   post of duty
> Till his soul was called
> To meet his God."

Ironically, the Little River Railroad helped contribute to the demise of logging in the Smokies and the creation of the national park. In 1909, LRLC started putting on regular weekend "excursion cars" for tourists and summer home owners at Elkmont. For the first time, many people were able to witness firsthand the scenic beauty of the park and the devastating effects of the clear-cutting conducted by the lumber companies. In 1927, LRLC became the first of the major timber companies in the Smokies to sell its land to the State of Tennessee for national park purposes. The company did, however, retain rights to continue logging until 1939. When the last logs passed through the Townsend Mill, the Little River Railroad made its final run and the piercing sound of a train whistle echoed through the Little River Gorge for the last time.

After the company pulled up its tracks, the Park service turned the railroad grade into the Little River Road, one of the most scenic drives in the Park. Other railroad grades in the Smokies were turned into roads or hiking trails and if visitors look closely they can see the rusty remains of logging equipment, railroad ties, and railroad spikes scattered in the undergrowth throughout the Park.

"The tracks are gone now. So are the mills, the towns, the camps, and the tannery. Ghostly remains of bygone days can be seen on roads and trails, woodland paths and forest meadows. Look! Hear the sound of the whistle over the mountain."
— Bill Hooks and Ronald Schmidt, authors of *Whistle Over the Mountain*

LITTLE RIVER RAILROAD Poster art based on a 27" x 36" oil painting created in 2017 by Kai Carpenter >

GREAT SMOKY MOUNTAINS
NATIONAL PARK
Cades Cove

Aaron J

Cades Cove

IF YOU HAVE ONLY one day in Great Smoky Mountains National Park and want to experience almost all of the pleasures the Park has to offer, then go to Cades Cove. The 11-mile Cades Cove Loop Road is perhaps the most scenic in the Park, featuring spectacular views of the mountains framing the open land and picturesque log cabins, barns, churches, cemeteries, and a grist mill. Cades Cove is also one of the best sites for viewing wildlife. It has mountain streams and waterfalls, offers both car camping and backpacking opportunities, and serves as trailhead for some of the Park's most iconic hikes. It is one of the most beloved areas of the Smokies as evidenced by the more than 2 million visitors who enjoy the area each year.

Cades Cove is an unusual geologic feature in the Southern Appalachian region called a limestone window. While there are similar sites in the region, none remotely approach the size and openness of Cades Cove. The weathering of the limestone over the years has also produced unusually deep and fertile soil which attracted early white pioneers despite the Cove's relative isolation.

While there is little evidence of permanent Native American sites in Cades Cove, the Cherokee did use it for seasonal hunting and gathering. The Cove was named for Chief Kade, a local leader among the Cherokee. White settlers began moving into the area as war and treaties pushed

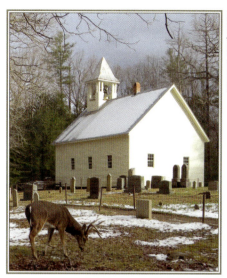

Cades Cove Primitive Baptist Church

the Cherokee out. John and Lucretia Oliver were the first white settlers in 1818, and the Oliver family remained influential in the Cove until the 1930s.

In Cades Cove, the National Park Service preserves many artifacts of the pioneer settlers and their lifestyle in the 19th century. One the Cove's major attractions is the opportunity to walk in and among the many log cabins (including John Oliver's), barns, outbuildings, churches, graveyards, and even a working over-shot wheel grist mill maintained there. Signage and interpretive guides help visitors better understand the history of both Cades Cove and the Southern Appalachian region.

Perhaps the biggest attraction in the Cove, however, is its abundance of wildlife. Cades Cove contains some of the largest populations of white tail deer, turkeys, and black bears you will ever

see. Visitors often have the opportunity to see them relatively up close in their natural habitat. Winter is an especially good time to see the white tail bucks battling it out with their massive antlers for dominance and the chance to breed with a harem of does. But it is not only the cove's "megafauna" like deer and bears that make this place special. Visitors who are willing to look closely might also see groundhogs, skunks, coyotes, bobcats, or even the very shy river otters that frequent Abrams Creek. The west end of Cades Cove also provides great opportunities for bird watching and, although they are not of the synchronous variety, the fireflies put on a great show here in early summer. Visitors need to be aware, however, that they are not at a petting zoo, that these are indeed wild animals which can hurt you, and that the Rangers are very serious about preventing the harassment or harming of any of the Park's wildlife.

A drive, bike, or hike around Cades Cove is one of the great pleasures afforded visitors to Great Smoky Mountains National Park. Prepare to be patient, use pull-offs to observe the scenery, historic sites, and wildlife, and be prepared for the almost inevitable deer or bear jams. The National Park Service recommends planning two to four hours for a trip around the loop road although it can take longer in the peak fall season or on summer weekends.

EXTRAS

HIKING HINT:
Five trailheads stem from the Loop. The busiest trails are Abrams Falls and Anthony Creek while the least used are Rabbit Creek and Cooper Road.

ROAD TRIP TIP:
If you don't want to make the entire 11-mile drive on the one-way Loop, be sure to take the shortcuts at Sparks Lane or Hyatt Lane for a quicker trip back out.

At Abrams Creek, look for
RIVER OTTERS

<CADES COVE 18" x 24" Poster art based on a digital painting created in 2017 by Aaron Johnson

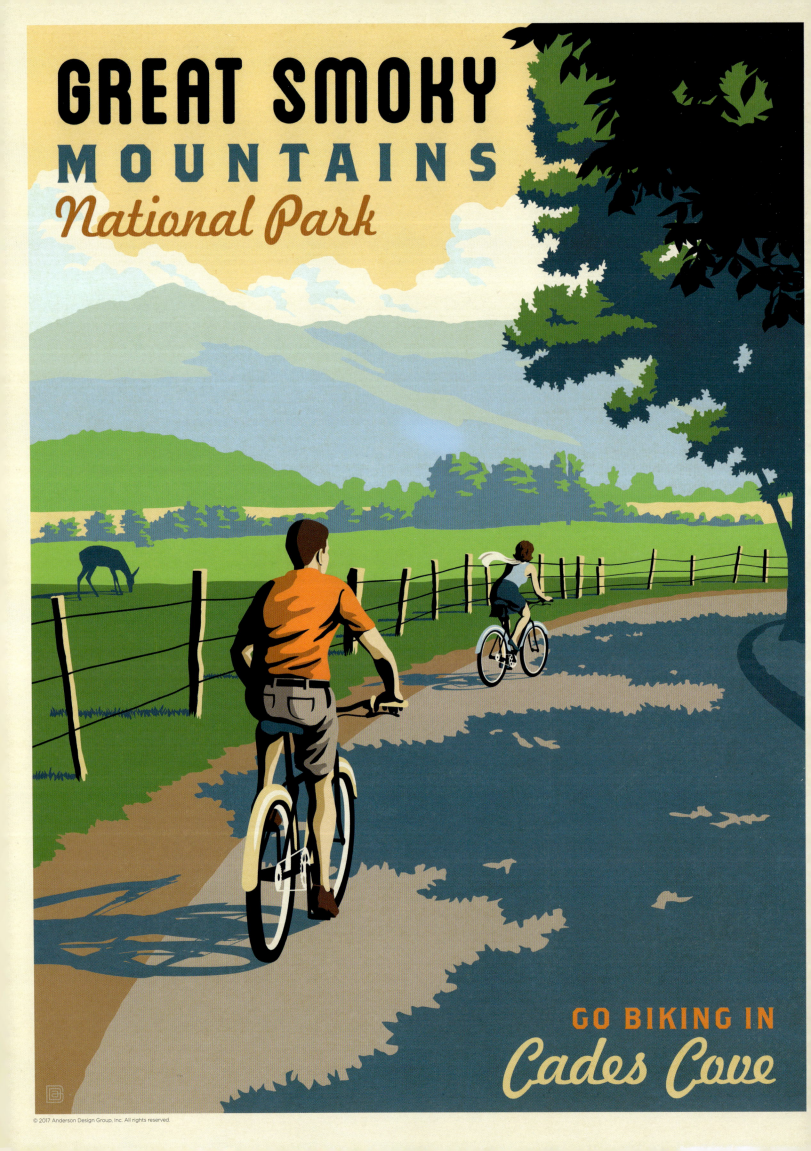

GREAT SMOKY
MOUNTAINS
National Park

GO BIKING IN
Cades Cove

Bicycle Riding in Cades Cove

ONE OF THE GREAT ways to enjoy the majestic scenery, wildlife, and historic sites of Cades Cove is to take a bike ride around the paved 11-mile Cades Cove Loop Road. While the road is often congested with cars, the National Park Service closes it to automobile traffic on Wednesdays and Saturdays from early May to late September until 10:00 a.m. to give priority to bikers and hikers. If visitors are not up for the 11-mile ride, which can get hilly in spots, they can shorten their trip by using the gravel bypass roads at Sparks Lane or Hyatt Lane.

Biking or hiking the Cove on a Wednesday or Saturday morning offers visitors the stunning views of Cades Cove in an environment of quiet and solitude, something visitors who drive the road in automobiles during peak visitation periods simply cannot experience. It also provides opportunities to observe the abundant deer, turkey, songbirds, and other wildlife without the crowds, backed up traffic, and jammed pull-offs characteristic of the road at high season.

Riding the Cove is a unique experience in the Smokies because opportunities for bicycle riding are relatively limited in the Park. All trails except Gatlinburg Trail, Oconaluftee River Trail, and the lower part of Deep Creek Trail are off-limits to bicycles. Bikes are allowed on the paved roads in the Park, but riding can be hazardous with narrow roads and heavy traffic. Adventurous road bikers may take on the challenge of the heart-pumping climb up, and the scream-inducing ride down, Newfound Gap Road to Newfound Gap (over 3,500 feet in 16.5 miles) or even to the Clingmans Dome parking lot, a climb of 5,300 feet over 23 miles. Lakeview Road, which travels 6.5 miles into the Park just outside the quaint town of Bryson City, NC, offers a less congested and a bit less challenging road biking experience in the Smokies. Bikers may also use the Roaring Fork Motor Nature Trail and Clingmans Dome, Heintoga, Straight Fork, Rich Mountain, and Parson Branch Roads when the gates are closed to automobile traffic in winter.

Opportunities for both mountain and road biking adventures do abound right outside the Park in both Tennessee and North Carolina. The world-famous Tsali system of mountain biking trails hugs the shoreline of North Carolina's Fontana Lake and offers lovely views of the Smokies. The town of Townsend has a relatively flat, paved, nine-mile bike trail that is appropriate for riders of all ages and fitness levels. Part of the trail runs along Little River providing great stream views.

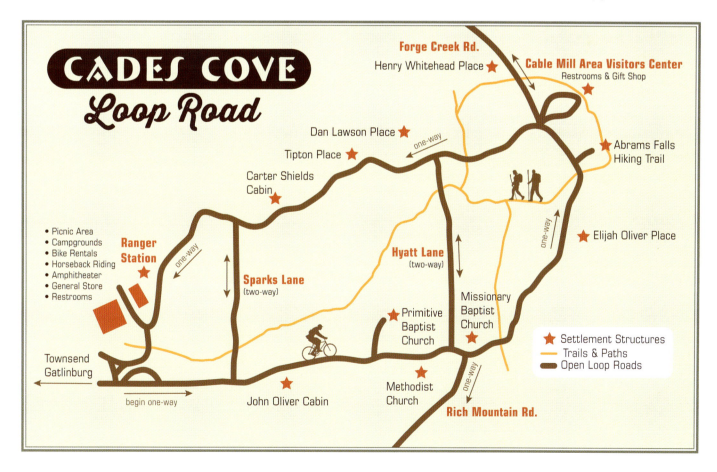

<BIKING IN CADES COVE 18" x 24" Poster art created in 2017 by Aaron Johnson & Joel Anderson

Gregory Bald

Flame Azaleas in full bloom on Gregory Bald

AT 4,949 FEET, Gregory Bald is one of the most striking examples of the grassy bald, a unique Southern Appalachian ecosystem. It is the largest bald in the Smokies and provides sweeping 360° views, most notably looking down 3,000 feet into Cades Cove. Gregory Bald is an especially popular destination in mid-June when the flame azaleas put on a stunning display of vibrant blooms. Pioneering environmentalist Harvey Broome described their "diverse hues, running from white through all the pinks, yellows, salmons, and flames, to deep saturated reds."

The origins of mountain balds are unclear. Most Smokies balds - like Spence Field, Andrews Bald, Silers Bald, and Maddron Bald - were probably formed as the result of human clearing by early European settlers in the 1800s who grazed thousands of cattle and sheep on the mountain tops in the summer months. Some, and most notably Gregory Bald, apparently preceded European settlement making their origins more mysterious. One sign of its probable pre-European origins is that Gregory figures prominently in old Cherokee folk tales as Tsistu'yi, or "Rabbit Place," home of the legendary trickster the Great Rabbit. In 1821, before significant European settlement in the area, explorer William Davenport observed two "bald spots" in the Smokies, the most likely candidates being Gregory Bald and Parson Bald. Scholars speculate that these balds may have been created by natural forces such as freezing and thawing, high winds, wildfire, or a combination of factors. The Cherokee may have maintained their grassy status as attractors for their favored game animals, particularly deer.

Once white settlers moved into Cades Cove, Gregory Bald was maintained by grazing cattle well into the 20th century. Cattlemen expanded the grassy areas by cutting trees and setting ground fires. The mountain is named for Russell Gregory, a noted Cades Cove farmer murdered by Confederate raiders in 1864. When the Smokies became a national park and grazing ceased, bushes and trees began to invade and cover the open areas. In order to preserve this unique landscape, the Park Service uses a variety of tactics, including mowing and burning, to keep Gregory Bald and Andrews Bald in their "bald" status.

Gregory Bald is only accessible to visitors via hiking trail. The shortest hike to the top is along Gregory Bald Trail at 4.5 miles, but Gregory Ridge Trail requires a much shorter drive to the trailhead and the trail is only 1.2 miles longer. While the June flame azalea season is the most popular time for a Gregory Bald hike, August offers a profusion of wild blueberries near the summit, and any clear day is a wonderful time to witness some of the most spectacular views in the Smokies.

EXTRAS

FUN FACT:
Forge Creek Road (which leads to the Gregory Bald Ridge trailhead) runs through Chestnut Flats, a pre-Park neighborhood that was once notorious for moonshine-related crime.

DID YOU KNOW?
Wild hogs are prolific in this area. Keep an eye out for patches of torn-up earth caused by their rooting snouts.

In June, look for the
FLAME AZALEA

GREGORY BALD 18" x 24" Poster art created in 2017 by Aaron Johnson & Joel Anderson >

SEE THE FLAME AZALEAS ATOP *Gregory Bald*

GREAT SMOKY
Mountains NATIONAL PARK

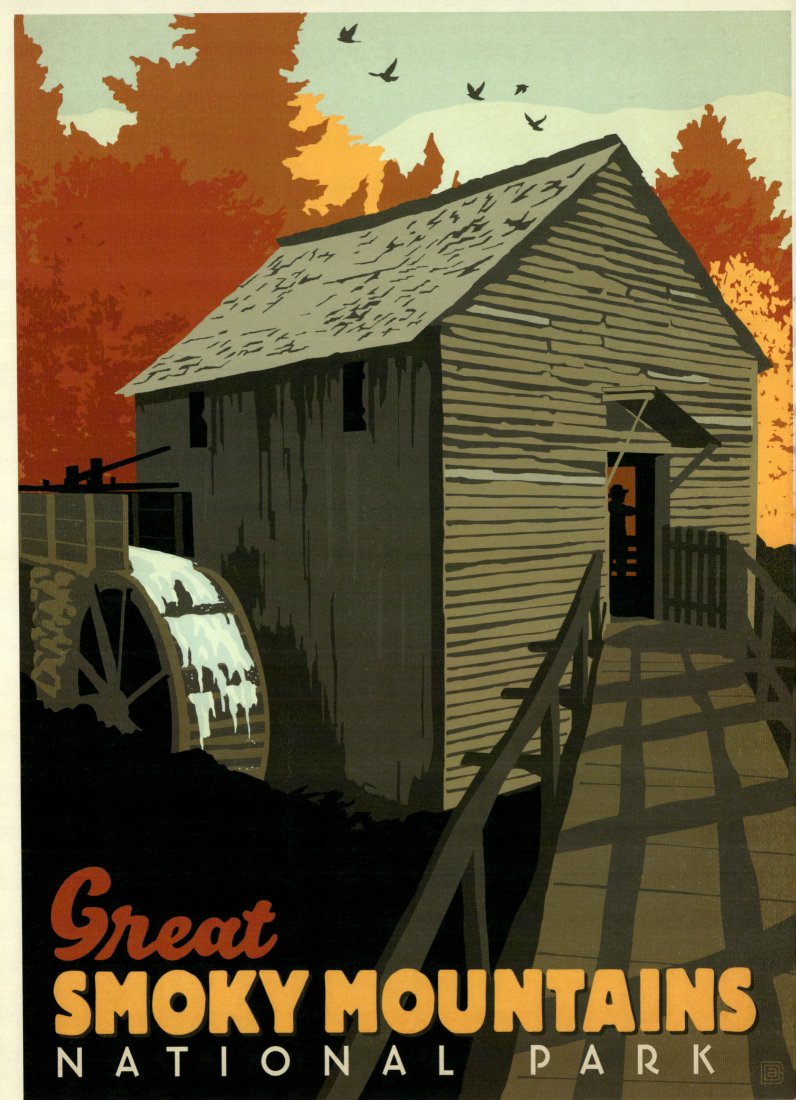

Great
SMOKY MOUNTAINS
NATIONAL PARK

Water-Powered Mills

WATER-POWERED grist mills were a key component of pioneer life in the Smokies. While many farmers in the area built small tub mills on creeks, by the late 19th century most communities had mills powered by overshot water wheels or water-powered turbines to grind the community's grain. Millers were compensated with a percentage of the ground meal known as the "miller's toll." Two large working mills are preserved in Great Smoky Mountains National Park for visitors to see in action: Mingus Mill near Oconaluftee and Cable Mill in Cades Cove.

Corn has been the staple of life in the Great Smoky Mountains for at least 1,000 years. For the Cherokee, corn was one of the sacred "Three Sisters" that also included beans and squash-related crops. The most important celebration of the year was the Green Corn Ceremony held in late summer. To grind it into meal for bread or porridge, the Cherokee placed their corn on large flat rocks and pounded it into meal using hand-held grinding stones. Europeans quickly saw the benefits of a local, nutritious grain well-adapted to

Cable Mill in Cades Cove

the environment and learned how to cultivate it from the natives. They soon became as dependent on corn as the Cherokee, adapting traditional uses of corn meal to their own tastes and soon corn bread, hoe cakes, grits, and hominy were an important part of their diet. The settlers also used corn meal to perpetuate their tradition of converting grains into alcohol and became adept at making potent corn liquor, a perfectly legal enterprise until the Civil War.

White settlers in the Smokies adapted Old World methods of grinding grain to their new circumstances and new staple crop. Many farms built small log turbine mills on nearby creeks to grind their grain. Visitors can see one of these on the loop trail behind Noah Bud Ogle's Cabin on Cherokee Orchard Road. By the mid-to-late 1800s, however, most of the grain grinding in the Smokies was done by large commercial mills. These large mills became centers of community life, particularly for the men who hauled corn, rye, wheat or barley to mill. While waiting for the miller to grind their grain, community members shared the latest news or gossip, talked politics, and swapped tall tales.

The Mingus Mill in the Oconaluftee area on the North Carolina side features an unusual turbine mill. The Cable Mill at the west end of Cades Cove was first constructed some time in the 1870s and features the classic overshot wheel most people are familiar with.

Tub Mill on Le Conte Creek

<**CABLE MILL** 18" x 24" Poster art created in 2017 by Michael Korfhage & Joel Anderson

Bear Jams

Photos by Open Parks Network

THE AMERICAN black bear has long been the signature animal for Great Smoky Mountains National Park and the Bear Jam - a line of cars backed up bumper-to-bumper with passengers ogling a black bear - has been a characteristic visitor experience of automobile tourists. Up until the late 1960s, the use of open trashcans at picnic areas and overlooks along the Park's busiest roads almost guaranteed a bear sighting, and a bear jam, for visitors. Since the installation of bearproof trashcans, however, bear jams occur less frequently. The Park does have an estimated population of 1,500 bears, so sightings and subsequent bear jams can still occur along any Park road.

The Great Smoky Mountains provide some of the best black bear habitat, and one of the largest contiguous protected areas, in the eastern United States. The mountains provide plenty of food for these omnivorous creatures. Over 80% of their diet comes from the profusion of nuts and berries that grow in the Park, although bears will eat a wide variety of plants, insects, or animal carrion when they find it. They do occasionally prey on smaller, relatively defenseless, animals as Park rangers discovered when bears began making a

significant dent in the survival rate of baby elk in the Cataloochee area.

Average male bears weigh around 250 pounds while females generally weigh a little more than 100 pounds. However, both can double their weight in the fall as they eat voraciously in preparation for denning up over winter, although they are not true hibernators. Some

mature male bears can get as large as six-feet long and 600 pounds. Mature female bears generally birth one to four cubs while in their dens. The cubs stay with, or near, their mothers for about 18 months. The best time to sight a bear is in the early morning or late evening when they are most active.

While they may look cute and cuddly, black bears are much stronger than humans, have sharp teeth and claws, can run as fast as a horse over short distances, and are skilled climbers. Visitors should avoid close encounters at all costs. Bears are also incredibly

resourceful, particularly when they are trying to get at food and especially in pursuit of a tourist's "pic-a-nic basket" (as cartoon character Yogi Bear called them). Visitors need to keep food away from and out of sight of bears and follow Park Service rules on food storage at overlooks, picnic areas, campgrounds, and backcountry campsites.

Black bears are generally not aggressive and in most cases will move away from you should you encounter one. If a bear changes its behavior, you are probably too close. If a bear moves toward you, make a lot of noise, make yourself appear as big as you can, and back away slowly. If in the extremely unlikely event that a bear attacks, fight back aggressively, do not play dead, and above all do not try to outrun it. Such bear encounters are extremely rare, but they do happen, so keep your food stored properly and keep your distance.

Although visitors often equate Smokey the Bear of "Only You Can Prevent Forest Fires" fame with the Great Smoky Mountains, there is no connection. Smokey was an orphaned bear cub rescued from a forest fire in New Mexico and the anti-wildfire campaign was one launched by the USDA Forest Service and not the National Park Service.

BEAR JAM Poster art based on a 27" x 36" oil painting created in 2017 by Kai Carpenter >

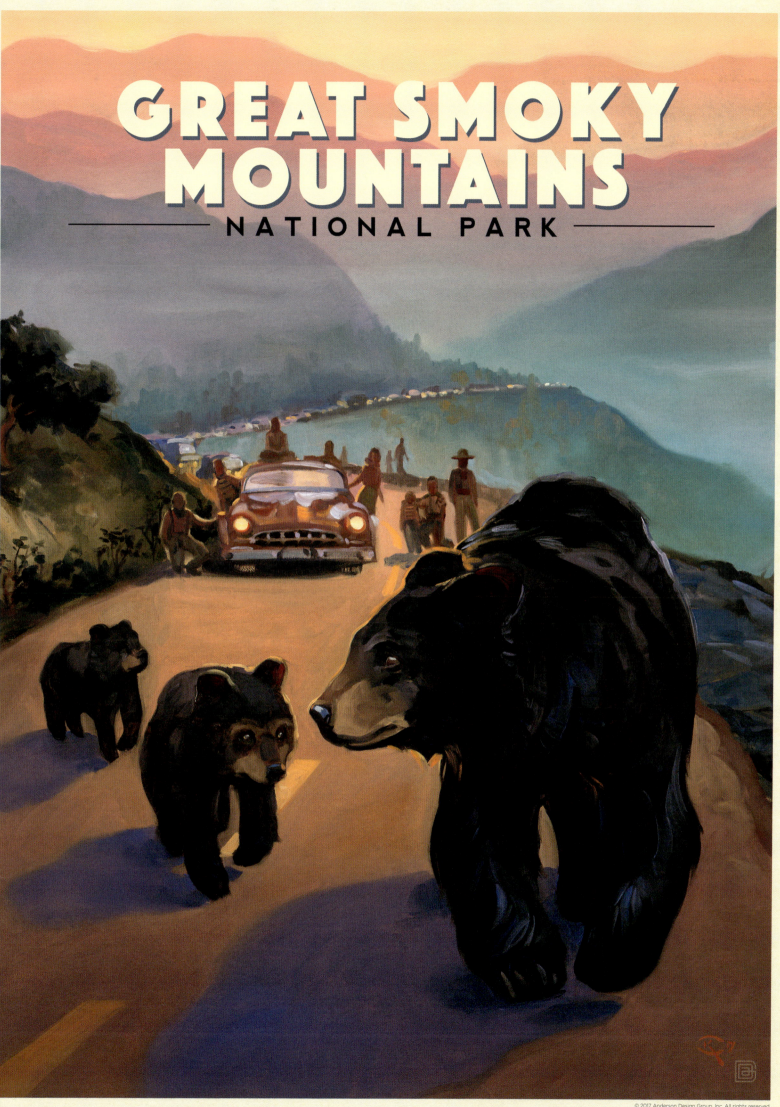

GREAT SMOKY
MOUNTAINS
— NATIONAL PARK —

GREAT SMOKY MOUNTAINS

Foothills Parkway

Foothills Parkway

Photo by Joel Anderson

Photo by Brian Schrayer

FOOTHILLS PARKWAY is a hidden gem of the Great Smoky Mountains. Few visitors even realize that the uncompleted 72-mile National Scenic Parkway is administered by Great Smoky Mountains National Park. The planned route for the scenic drive runs from Highway 129 in the far western end of the Park near Chilhowee Lake all the way to Interstate 40 near Cosby, roughly paralleling the Park's northern boundary. Currently 5.6 miles on its eastern end connect I-40 and U.S. Highway 321 at Cosby and a 16.9-mile section connects U.S. Highway 129 at Chilhowee Lake with Highway 321 at Walland. The 3.5-mile Gatlinburg Spur connecting Pigeon Forge and Gatlinburg is also a part of the Parkway. A 15.8-mile section connecting Walland to Wears Valley is currently nearing completion.

The current open sections of the Parkway offer a relaxing alternative to the crowded roads of the Park itself. The western end runs along the Chilhowee Mountains and provides wonderful views of the Smokies on one side and the Unicoi Mountains and Tennessee River Valley on the other. The eastern end of the Parkway rises from I-40, crosses a ridge and descends to Cosby Creek. Overlooks on its eastern end provide views of Webb Mountain and the Pigeon River Valley while the ride from the top of the mountain to Cosby offers the best long-range views of the eastern Great Smokies ridgeline and its most prominent peaks: Mount Cammerer, Cosby Knob, and Mount Guyot.

The soon-to-be opened Walland to Wears Valley section is one of the Parkway's most scenic areas. Often referred to as its "missing link," the rugged terrain of this section has challenged engineers and builders and required the construction of 10 bridges in a single 1.6-mile stretch. It should be one of the most popular scenic drives in the area when it opens. Bridge #2 on Foothills Parkway is a spectacular structure that gracefully hugs the side of the mountain. This innovative bridge made of precast concrete is similar to the Blue Ridge Parkway's world-famous Lynn Cove Viaduct on Grandfather Mountain and is designed to blend into the mountain scenery.

As of publication of this book, this section of the Parkway is still under construction and is scheduled to open in 2019.

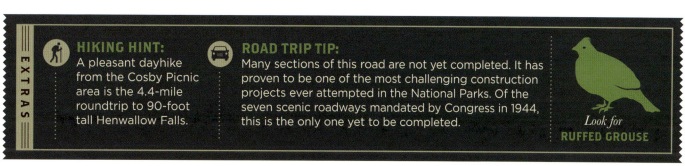

EXTRAS

🥾 **HIKING HINT:**
A pleasant dayhike from the Cosby Picnic area is the 4.4-mile roundtrip to 90-foot tall Henwallow Falls.

🚙 **ROAD TRIP TIP:**
Many sections of this road are not yet completed. It has proven to be one of the most challenging construction projects ever attempted in the National Parks. Of the seven scenic roadways mandated by Congress in 1944, this is the only one yet to be completed.

Look for
RUFFED GROUSE

<FOOTHILLS PARKWAY 18" x 24" Poster art created in 2017 by Derek Anderson & Joel Anderson

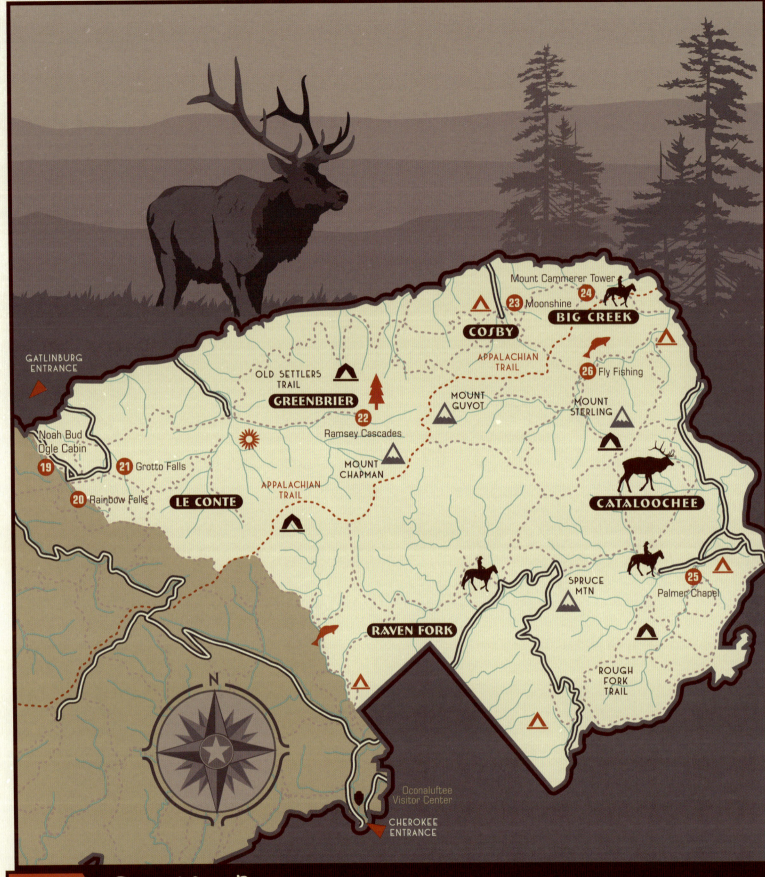

Gatlinburg Entrance

Noah Bud Ogle Cabin

19

21 Grotto Falls

20 Rainbow Falls

LE CONTE

APPALACHIAN TRAIL

OLD SETTLERS TRAIL

GREENBRIER

22

Ramsey Cascades

MOUNT CHAPMAN

MOUNT GUYOT

COSBY

23 Moonshine

Mount Cammerer Tower

24

BIG CREEK

APPALACHIAN TRAIL

26 Fly Fishing

MOUNT STERLING

CATALOOCHEE

RAVEN FORK

SPRUCE MTN

Palmer Chapel

25

ROUGH FORK TRAIL

N

Oconaluftee Visitor Center

CHEROKEE ENTRANCE

PART 3 *The Wild East*

The Eastern Third of the Park (Roaring Fork to Raven Fork)

Photos by Joel Anderson

The eastern section of Great Smoky Mountains National Park—Gatlinburg to Cherokee—has some of the most remote and rugged terrain in the eastern United States. This area contains much of the Park's old-growth forests and hosts amazing biological diversity as well as some of the areas most spectacular wildflower displays. While it is remote, this Smokies wilderness is accessible via several roads (many unpaved). Make sure to check for road conditions as some of these roads will close in the winter. Don't let rugged conditions keep you away as a visit to the "Wild East" will be rewarded with sights you rarely see elsewhere.

The Roaring Fork Motor Nature Road is your starting point for two gorgeous waterfall hikes: Rainbow Falls and Grotto Falls. Rainbow Falls, a scenic rest stop that was once enjoyed by Smoky Jack and Paul Adams on their trips up to Mount Le Conte, is a somewhat strenuous 2.7-mile hike. Grotto Falls, a 1.3-mile hike, is a wonderful spot to see wildflowers and hunt for salamanders.

Visitors can learn about pioneer life at the historic Noah Bud Ogle Cabin from Roaring Fork as well.

Greenbrier Road plunges into the an-

cient forests of the eastern Smokies. From the end of this road, take a 4-mile hike up to Ramsey Cascades where water joyfully tumbles from rock to rock 100 feet down into the gorge.

The Cosby Entrance Road transports you to a Smoky Mountain paradise known not only for its natural beauty but for its rich moonshine history and Civilian Conservation Corps feats of engineering, such as the Mount Cammerer Tower.

The oft-overlooked Big Creek Road provides a delightful escape into solitude right off Interstate 40. You will have Midnight Hole and Mouse Creek Falls practically to yourself during the off-season. Fly fishermen should don their hiking boots if they want a chance to catch a speckled trout, rehabilitated natives to the Big Creek region.

Bring some dramamine if you're riding backseat up Cove Creek Road. The switchbacks might make you nauseous but the views from Cataloochee are pristine (be sure to stop at Palmer Chapel). Large herds of elk often graze here during the evenings as well.

Heintoga and Straight Fork Roads slice into pristine wilderness east of Newfound Gap. Fly fishing and animal watching opportunities abound here. One of our favorite backcountry spots, Raven Fork, is located in these remote highlands northwest of Balsam Mountain. Though a difficult hike, those that venture into Raven Fork will be given access to an Appalachian Eden untouched by time or mankind.

Noah Bud Ogle Cabin

Photos by Joel Anderson

THE NOAH BUD OGLE

Cabin and Farmstead provide Park visitors with a visual history of the way white settlers lived in the Smokies for much of the 19th century. Noah Ogle (1863 - 1913) was a descendent of one of the first white settlers in the Gatlinburg area. He once owned 400 acres where he supported his family with a variety of subsistence and commercial activities. The site contains Ogle's cabin, a four-pen barn, a one-mile nature trail, and a small turbine (or "tub" mill) used to grind corn on nearby Le Conte Creek.

Ogle's "saddlebag" cabin is unique to the Smokies and is actually composed of two cabins which share a central chimney. The second cabin was added on when Ogle's family outgrew the single room. In order to accommodate a large family, each cabin also had a loft where children commonly slept. The cabin has wide covered porches running along the front and the back where family members spent much of their leisure time during the warmer months sharing stories and gossip, visiting with neighbors, breaking beans or shucking corn, even singing old ballads or popular songs together. The yard would have been alive with chickens, geese, and maybe a guinea hen or two, with at least a couple of dogs lazing under the porch.

The four-pen barn indicates the importance of livestock on Ogle's farm and sheltered his milk cows and draft animals. Much of his subsistence and market activity would have been based on livestock such as cattle and hogs that free-ranged the mountains during much of the year. During Ogle's heyday, the woods around his home teemed with foraging hogs. These were not the typical hogs we think of today, but small, lean, and hairy creatures equipped with razor sharp tusks. Writer Horace Kephart described the hogs he encountered in the Smokies:

"Shaped in front like a thin wedge, he can go through laurel thickets like a bear. Armored with tough hide cushioned with bristles, he despises thorns, brambles, and rattlesnakes alike. His extravagantly long snout can scent like a cat's, and yet burrow, uproot, overturn, as if made of metal. The long legs, thin flanks, pliant hoofs, fit him to run like a deer and climb like a goat."

Smokies farmers also grazed cattle on mountain balds in the summer, fattening them on the rich grasses. In the fall, they drove their excess cattle and hogs to market, most often to Knoxville. The cash money they received paid their property taxes and enabled them to purchase store bought goods like coffee, metal tools,

and sugar. In the fall, they killed several hogs, processed them into ham, sausage, bacon, and lard, then smoked the meat and stored it for winter.

A walk along the Nature Trail takes the visitor through the land that Ogle once farmed. Seeing all the rocks scattered amongst the trees gives one an idea of the challenges Smokies farmers faced trying to plow, sow, hoe, and reap. While corn composed most of Ogle's crop, he also grew the crops common to the Cherokee such as beans, squashes, melons, and gourds. Farmers in the area also grew potatoes, onions, cabbage, and other crops brought from Europe. Ogle also had a large apple orchard. Much of the apple crop would have probably been made into cider, much easier to transport to market and much more profitable.

The trail walk also takes you by Le Conte Creek and Ogle's tub mill where he ground his corn and other grains and even made a little profit by charging neighbors a portion of their meal in exchange for his milling services. At one time there were probably a dozen other such mills along this creek alone.

The Ogle place provides the visitor with an up-close look at a lifestyle that predominated in the Smokies for much of the 1800s and persisted with some families into the 20th century.

NOAH BUD OGLE CABIN 18" x 24" Poster art created by Derek Anderson & Joel Anderson in 2017 >

Great
SMOKY
MOUNTAINS
NOAH BUD OGLE CABIN

Rainbow Falls

RAINBOW FALLS is an 83-foot waterfall on the slopes of Mount Le Conte, the longest single drop for a waterfall in the Smokies. Because Le Conte Creek is relatively small above the falls, water tends to flow as a mist over the cliff. Light diffusing through the mist on sunny afternoons casts rainbow hues on the rock wall, giving the waterfall its name.

The falls are accessible via Rainbow Falls Trail which begins near the end of Cherokee Orchard Road, just above the Noah Bud Ogle homestead. Due to the popularity of the falls and the fact that the trail is one of the easier access trails to Mount Le Conte, the parking area can fill on weekends and at peak seasons.

At such times, it is advisable to arrive early. The roundtrip hike to Rainbow Falls and back is a rocky and muddy 5.6 miles and involves climbing almost 2,000 feet. Hiking all the way to the top of Mount Le Conte requires another 3.9-mile trek.

Hikers, however, are well rewarded for their efforts. The trail runs for much of its length along Le Conte Creek offering beautiful streamside views. This area receives some of the highest amounts of rainfall in the nation and, since the trail runs on the north side of Mount Le Conte, stays damp except under extreme drought. As a result, visitors can witness firsthand one of the great success stories of the Smokies and of the National Park System in general: a hardwood forest which has almost recovered its old-growth status after being clear-cut by loggers less than a century ago. The forest is different from the original old-growth forest of the early 20th century, to be sure. The chestnuts that once dominated it are long gone (although old chestnut logs still rot on the forest floor and shoots still sprout out of old root systems) and now most of the hemlocks are dead and dying, but it is still a magnificent sight. This trail is also a wonderful wildflower trail from spring to fall. Visitors can see trilliums, turtleheads, crimson bee-balm, yellow coneflowers, pink lady's slippers and dozens of other varieties along the way.

Rainbow Falls is particularly spectacular in very cold weather and is a reminder that some of the best hiking in the Park comes in winter. When the Smokies get a long cold snap, the mist flowing over the falls freezes and creates a cone of bluish ice at the bottom and a jagged fringe of ice hanging from the brink of the falls. In extended cold spells the two can join to form a stunning pillar of ice. Harvey Broome described the wonder of this sight in his book *Out Under the Skies of the Great Smokies*: "In color it was a delicate icy blue. This color was almost unbelievable - almost luminescent, almost vanishing, but real enough in its subtle beauty."

Photos by Open Parks Network

RAINBOW FALLS 18" x 24" Poster art created by Derek Anderson & Joel Anderson in 2017 >

GREAT SMOKY
MOUNTAINS NATIONAL PARK

Rainbow Falls

GREAT SMOKY MOUNTAINS
GROTTO FALLS

Aaron J.

Grotto Falls

DESPITE BEING a relatively small waterfall with only a 25-foot cascade, Grotto Falls is a beautiful sight in a spectacular setting. A lovely 2.6-mile roundtrip hike along Trillium Gap Trail will take you to the only waterfall in the Park where visitors can walk behind the falls. The area provides numerous places to spot iconic Smokies salamanders who love the cool, damp environment. Trillium Gap Trail is one of the six trails that provide access to the summit of Mount Le Conte.

The shortest way to access the falls is from the Grotto Falls parking area along the Roaring Fork Motor Nature Trail, but when that road is closed during the winter, hikers can take the longer route from the Trillium Gap Trailhead on Cherokee Orchard Road. Either way, the trail offers a number of special treats providing a

cool and pleasant streamside hike along Roaring Fork through an old-growth forest of huge basswoods, beeches, and Fraser magnolias. Wildflowers also proliferate along the trail and in spring the trail is lined with white and yellow trilliums, squawcorn, and dutchman's breeches.

Along this trail visitors will hike through groves of an iconic Smoky Mountains tree, the Carolina Silverbell. For most of its range in upland areas of the Southeast, the silverbell appears as a shrub or a small tree rarely growing taller than 35 feet. In the Grotto Falls area, silverbells reach a height of up to 90 feet. The tree has two major distinctions which make it easy to identify. First, it has a distinctive shaggy bark that naturalist Steve Kemp ably describes: "It tends to flake in rough, rectangular, purple or blue-black

scales that bear a certain resemblance to a milk-chocolate bar." Indeed, some refer to it as the "Hershey tree." The silverbell's other distinctive feature is its white, bell-shaped blooms which can be as long as two inches. From late March to May the trail to Grotto Falls is especially delightful as parts of it are literally carpeted with fallen silverbell flowers. Because of its distinctive blooms, the silverbell is also known as the "snowdrop tree."

The hike to Grotto Falls is perfect for children and is especially refreshing on a hot summer's day. It offers great opportunities for nature study with its old-growth forest, wildflower displays, and is a great area for splashing in the creek and turning over rocks looking for stream creatures. If you're lucky you may also spot the llama train that takes supplies up to LeConte Lodge three times a week.

Photos by Joel Anderson

Carolina Silverbell

< GROTTO FALLS 18" x 24" Poster art based on a digital painting created in 2017 by Aaron Johnson

Salamander
CAPITAL OF THE WORLD!

Great
SMOKY MOUNTAINS
NATIONAL PARK

Salamanders

Blueridge Two-lined Salamander

Red-cheeked Salamander

WHEN THINKING OF wildlife in the Great Smoky Mountains visitors most often think of the black bear, the elk of Cataloochee and Oconaluftee, or the huge white-tail deer of Cades Cove. However, they ought to think of the most plentiful, most diverse (with over 30 species), and perhaps the most interesting vertebrate in the Park: the salmander. Indeed, naturalists often refer to the Smokies as the "Salamander Capital of the World."

The Smokies provide prime habitat for both large numbers of salamanders (locally known as "spring lizards") and a wide diversity of species. Several species of these creatures, including the Imitator Salamander and the Red-Cheeked Salamander, are only found within the confines of the Park. Salamanders range in size from the Pygmy Salamander, which are generally under two inches in length, to the Hellbender which can grow to more than two feet. They also come in a huge variety of colors and color patterns. While most salamanders have a dusky, brown color (the most common variety are the Dusky Salamanders), others have brilliant colors. The Mud Salamander sports a pinkish-orange color with dark spots, while the red-cheeked salamander appropriately has red cheeks which stand out against its primary color of iridescent blue. Some come with spots, some stripes, and some have mottled, camouflage-type color patterns.

Salamanders can be found in every stream and damp area in the Smokies and at every elevation. Some of them, like the huge Hellbender, spend their entire lives in water while others are totally terrestrial. The slimy Salamander group secretes a sticky slime that makes them unappetizing to predators. The lungless salamanders, who exchange oxygen and carbon dioxide through blood vessels in their skin, are especially plentiful in the park with 24 separate species.

Finding salamanders in the Park is relatively easy and hunting for them is a fun and memorable activity for children. Shallow streams like Roaring Fork and their edges are probably the best places to see them, but you can find them on the edges of larger streams like Little River or the Oconaluftee River, and you can even look under the leaves in damp forests. The same rules apply for salamanders as they do for larger wildlife in the Park. You can get closer to one than you do to a bear, deer, or elk, but they should not be handled. Also make sure not to remove rocks from the stream, you can usually see them peeking out from under the edges of rocks or fallen logs without displacing anything. A variety of guides for exploring the natural world are available at the Park's visitors centers.

< Poster: Black-chinned Red Salamander

EXTRAS

FUN FACT:
Salamanders and skinks may look similar, but salamanders are amphibians, while skinks are reptiles. Skinks have scales and claws, salamanders are clawless and have smooth, slimy skin.

GREAT RESOURCE:
Be sure to grab a copy of *Reptiles & Amphibians of the Smokies* from the Park bookstore. The book even includes a checklist to encourage you to find them all!

Look for
BLACK-BELLIED SALAMANDERS

<SALAMANDER 18" x 24" Poster art created in 2017 by Derek Anderson & Joel Anderson

GREAT SMOKY MOUNTAINS
NATIONAL PARK

Wildflower Heaven

Wildflowers

Crested Dwarf Iris

Yellow Trillium

Robin's Plantain

Photos by Joel Anderson

ONE FANTASTIC REASON to visit Great Smoky Mountains National Park is to witness the colorful displays of wildflowers that enliven almost any hike in the Park from early spring to late fall. There are over 1,500 varieties of flowering plants in the Smokies, the richest diversity of such plants in any North American national park. Scientists attribute this diversity to the Park's dramatic changes in elevation that produce a wide variety of habitats, to the abundance of rainfall, and to the relatively temperate climate.

The spring ephemeral wildflowers are particularly beautiful in the Smokies with a profusion of trilliums, Solomon Seal, pink lady's slippers, dwarf iris, jack-in-the-pulpit, and fire pinks lining the low to mid-elevation trails. With ten different species in the Park, the trilliums, with their large tri-petal blooms, and a range of color from bright white in the white trilliums to deep red in the wake robin, are particularly popular among visitors. These spring ephemerals appear in forest environments, emerge from the soil in early spring before the trees leaf out, and are gone by late May or early June. A great way to experience the spring wildflowers in the Smokies is to attend the Wildflower Pilgrimage held in Gatlinburg in April every year. The Pilgrimage features seminars and lectures on wildflowers as well as very popular wildflower hikes that take participants into the Smokies to see the colorful displays firsthand.

While generally not as showy, wildflower displays continue until late fall. In summer visitors often see the bright red blooms of bee-balm and cardinal flower and the vibrant oranges of the Turk's cap lily and jewel weed, especially in moist environments. Fall features the

Thyme-leaved Bluets

more subdued, but still beautiful blooms of coneflowers, asters, mountain gentian, and monk's hood.

Some variety of wildflower grows on every trail in the Smokies but a few trails are known especially for their spring wildflowers. Porters Creek Trail, Bradley Creek Trail, Little River Trail, Rich Mountain Loop, Chestnut Top/Schoolhouse Gap Trail, and the Cosby and Cove Hardwood Nature Trails all have the reputation for consistently spectacular displays. Visitors can also see lovely displays of wildflowers from their cars along the Roaring Fork Motor Nature Trail near Gatlinburg and Rich Mountain and Balsam Mountain Roads. Wildfires, particularly low-intensity ground fires, can actually benefit some species of wildflowers, such as those in the aster and orchid families that thrive on drier slopes.

Like all resources in the Park, wildflowers are protected and visitors cannot pick them or dig them up to transplant at home.

EXTRAS

⭐ **FUN FACT:** The first half-mile of Chestnut Top Trail is a wildflower bonanza with 40+ species blooming in the springtime.

ℹ **GREAT RESOURCE:** *Wildflowers of the Smokies* (available in Park bookstores) is an excellent handbook for identifying the Park's vast variety of flowering plants. The book will help you appreciate not only a plant's flowers, but its stem, leaf shape, and patterns too.

In low elevations, look for **ROBIN'S PLANTAIN**

‹WILDFLOWER HEAVEN Poster art based on a 30" x 40" acrylic painting created in 2017 by Joel Anderson

Ramsey Cascades

GREAT SMOKY MOUNTAINS
NATIONAL PARK

Ramsey Cascades

AT ALMOST 100 FEET, Ramsey Cascades is the highest waterfall in Great Smoky Mountains National Park. Appropriately, given its name, the waterfall cascades in stair-step fashion over boulders collecting in a small pool at the bottom. Getting to Ramsey Cascades requires a 4-mile relatively strenuous hike along Ramsey Prong and through an old-growth forest.

Ramsey Cascades lies in the Greenbrier section and the road to the trailhead enters the Park just outside Gatlinburg's eastern city limits off of U.S. Highway 321. The road travels through an area that was once home to a thriving community, one of the largest in what became the Park. The only evidences today of the Greenbrier neighborhood are crumbling foundations of homes, derelict rock walls that once surrounded corn fields, and the occasional rusting piece of metal from a washtub left behind when the inhabitants were forced to move in the 1930s.

Not far up Ramsey Cascades Trail, the visitor enters an ancient old-growth forest. The trail is particularly beautiful here as you pass through an open forest filled with massive tuliptrees, basswoods, and oaks. Here you'll also find near-record breaking white oak, red maple, black cherry, and silverbell trees. This opulent forest produces such grand trees because it is located on the north-facing slope of the main ridge of the Smokies. The north slope receives an enormous amount of rainfall, stays in the shade for much of the day, and remains damp at all seasons. Fortunately, the loggers of Champion Fibre Co. did not reach this area before the Company sold the land to the State of Tennessee for inclusion in the Park.

In the midst of this magnificent forest, however, visitors can also witness the damage done to the area's eastern hemlocks by the invasive hemlock wooly adelgid. The tiny insect arrived in the Park in 2002 and has decimated many 500+ year old trees, some that have grown to over 150 feet with trunks measuring over six-feet in diameter. While the Park service has treated some trees, particularly in more accessible areas, so that there will be a remnant population, the Ramsey Cascades area has seen a major ecological change in a very short period. Time will tell what the long-term impact is on this magical place.

The last part of the trail involves a steep scramble through boulders to reach the falls. The strenuous hike is rewarded with the sight of the cascading falls in the midst of a true wilderness and the roar of water tumbling off the rocks.

While you are in the midst of a wilderness, visitors do need to exercise the usual precautions around waterfalls and need to keep an eye on their backpacks. Due to the fact that Ramsey Cascades receives a lot of visitors who either intentionally or inadvertently feed the wildlife, red squirrels (called "boomers" in the Smokies) and other scavengers may try to find a free meal. I once had an up-close encounter with a yearling bear who was intent on getting to my pack while I sat reading a book at the base of the falls. Fortunately, after staring at one another for a few minutes, the young bear headed back into the forest, although I had concerns that its mother might show up at any moment!

Photos by Open Parks Network

Look for the **VEERY**

<RAMSEY CASCADES 18" x 24" Poster art created in 2017 by Aaron Johnson and Joel Anderson

Old-Growth Forests
GREAT SMOKY
MOUNTAINS
NATIONAL PARK

Old-Growth Forests

MOST VISITORS to Great Smoky Mountains National Park will witness the awesome views from ridges, mountain tops, and road overlooks. They'll enjoy the history, wildlife, and sweeping vistas of Cades Cove. They might marvel at the majesty of a bull elk at Oconaluftee or listen to the murmuring of the Park's creeks and rivers. But many miss out on seeing one of the great treasures of the Park: its groves of majestic old-growth forest. Over 100 species of trees grow in the Smokies, more than any other national park in North America, and with a little effort visitors have the opportunity to see many of these species at their peak size.

While most of the Park's forests were heavily logged and clear cut in the late 19th and early 20th centuries, Great Smoky Mountains National Park still contains almost 100,000 acres of old-growth forest that evaded the axe and cross-cut saw of the woodhicks (as loggers were called in the Smokies). The most impressive of the trees in these untouched areas are the tuliptrees (commonly called tulip poplars, although the tree is not a true poplar). These trees can reach massive dimensions with one giant along the Albright Grove Trail measuring 25-feet in circumference and another in the area reaching 191.9 feet in height. In the Smokies, however, visitors can see record-breaking hardwood trees such as white ash, black locust, American sycamore, a wide variety of

Photo by Joel Anderson

hickories, maples, and oaks, black walnut, basswood, beech, black and yellow birch, black cherry, cucumber tree, Fraser magnolia, yellow buckeye, sweetgum, Carolina silverbell, and sourwood. Old-growth stands of evergreen trees can also be found in the Smokies, especially the Fraser firs and red spruce at high elevations. The Boogerman Pine in the Cataloochee area was measured at 207 feet in height in 1995, a record for the eastern United States. Lightning later struck the tree and it lost a good bit of its top and its record.

Visitors should also notice the lush understory present in large stands of old-growth. The forest floor is covered with a wide variety of mosses and ferns and low-running shrubs like partridge

berry. Dead and decaying nurse logs - even some huge chestnuts which died more than 80 years ago - lie on the ground, enriching the soil and providing a nursery for ferns, mosses, lichen, and sprouting plants. This understory acts as a highly efficient filter which keeps sediment out of nearby streams. Even in heavy rain storms, the creeks running through old-growth still display a brilliant blue-green color and run clear.

Small patches of old-growth can be found throughout the Park, but some sites offer especially spectacular stands. The most accessible area is on the Cove Hardwood Nature Trail that starts in the Chimneys Picnic Area off of Newfound Gap Road. The Greenbrier area has the largest stands of old-growth in the Park but getting to the best areas requires a hike along Ramsey Cascades Trail or Maddron Bald Trail to Albright Grove. Impressive sections of old-growth can also be found on Baxter Creek Trail in Big Creek and on Boogerman Loop in Cataloochee.

Old-growth forests are one of the rarest ecosystems in the eastern United States, and the Great Smoky Mountains have more acres of them than any other area this side of the Mississippi River. Stepping into one of these primeval forests is an encounter with the awe-inspiring power of nature. There is a quiet connection with the eternal here that one will not soon forget.

<**OLD-GROWTH FORESTS** 18" x 24" Poster art created in 2017 by Derek Anderson & Joel Anderson

Moonshine

THE CRAFT OF WHISKEY

making was brought to the Smokies by white settlers, particularly those whose ancestors hailed from the British Isles. Selling and trading corn whiskey and brandy made from apples, peaches, and other fruits was an important, and perfectly legal, source of cash income for many Smoky Mountain families before the Civil War. When the federal excise tax of 1862 and later prohibition laws made the practice illegal, many inhabitants of the region continued (despite or to spite the law) to ply their craft in the hidden coves of the mountains, often at night by the light of the moon. In the Smokies these early illegal distillers were most commonly known as blockaders or moonshiners.

Distilling illegal liquor remained an essential part of economic and social life for many Smokies residents up until the 1960s and has continued to

the present day, although on a much smaller scale. There were many reasons folks chose to defy the law and make whiskey. Most often, the reasons were economic as mountain farmers faced a daunting environment in the post-Civil War years. Making moonshine was the surest way to earn cash money. Farmers often resorted to the practice temporarily in times of economic emergency or as young men to raise capital to get started in life. Ironically, one of the primary reasons many made liquor was that they needed cash to pay their property taxes and hold onto their mountain farms; in essence they were evading a federal tax in order to pay a county tax. Although many residents of the Smokies sided with the Union in the Civil War, it was also a way to defy the federal government and assert what they believed to be their God-given right to "make a little likker."

Of course this practice attracted the attention of law enforcement, with most of that enforcement coming from agents of the U.S. Treasury Department's Alcohol Tax Unit - generally known as "revenuers" in the mountains - and not from local law enforcement. Although the stereotypical accounts of moonshiners revel in stories of violent confrontations and shootouts with revenue agents (and these did happen on occasions), relationships between agents and moonshiners were generally civil, even cordial. Indeed both sides operated based on a code that required revenuers to physically catch the moonshiner at the still or in possession of illegal liquor. If agents could do that, and this was difficult, the moonshiner came along peaceably. In fact, on many occasions agents just told the captured blockader to show up in federal court on a particular date and they generally did.

"Most of the time if I found a still I'd leave a note on it and tell them to get it out by a certain date or we'd take care of it."
— Audley Whaley, ranger in the moonshine hotbeds of Cataloochee, Big Creek, and Cosby in the 1930s

<MOONSHINER Poster art based on a 27" x 36" oil painting created in 2017 by Kai Carpenter

When prohibition came to North Carolina and Tennessee (first on a local level, then statewide well before national prohibition in 1920), local law enforcement became more involved. However, local officials in the Smokies were rarely enthusiastic about enforcement as the moonshiners were often neighbors or even kin, and all of them were voters. At election time local sheriffs might make a few show busts for the benefit of the local town Baptists, but the moonshiners were often forewarned and had taken the most valuable parts of their stills and hidden them, leaving officials with token equipment that they could axe and haul to the county seat as trophies.

This points to a rather curious relationship between the forces of propriety and the illegal moonshine operation. While almost all of the churches in the region preached teetotaling abstinence from all alcoholic beverages, rural churches and their ministers understood the economic quandary many of their members faced and quietly tolerated moonshining. Legendary Smokies ranger Glen Cardwell, who grew up in the Greenbrier area, recollected his father's moonshining activities as part of the way he fed and clothed his family. Cardwell's father was a respected deacon in the local Baptist church, never drank, and his best customer was the Sevier County sheriff. The sheriff often pulled up to the Cardwell home in his squad car and loaded the trunk with moonshine. Popcorn Sutton, who moonshined on both sides of the Smokies averred that his granddaddy "Little" Mitch Sutton used the proceeds of a run of illegal liquor to purchase building materials for the first Baptist church constructed in the Hemphill Bald area.

Over the years the Smokies have produced and harbored some of the most

(in)famous moonshiners in history. Lewis Redmond, the purported "King of the Moonshiners" in the 1880s, had family roots in the Smokies in Swain County, North Carolina. When federal agents cracked down on the moonshine empire he had established in Upstate South Carolina, Redmond retreated to the mountains near Bryson City where he was captured in 1882. His (greatly exaggerated) escapades were profiled in

national newspapers such as the New York Times and in two widely distributed, and totally fanciful, dime novels. Quill Rose had a fifty-plus year career as

a moonshiner on Eagle Creek and successfully evaded law enforcement until he was busted in 1911 at the age of 70. Rose featured prominently in a couple of nationally distributed books on life and culture in the Smokies, most no-

tably in Horace Kephart's *Our Southern Highlanders*. Ike Costner of the Cosby section of Cocke County, Tennessee was one of the most notorious moonshiners in the history of the region with a career from the 1920s to the 1960s. Costner lived out the legend of "Thunder Road," hauling liquor out of the mountains in souped-up automobiles. He also demonstrates the costs of his career choice as he spent a sizeable amount of time incarcerated in federal penitentiaries from Ft. Levenworth, Kansas to Alcatraz. Costner did take advantage of his time behind bars, however, and took correspondence courses in law and business which made him both a skilled jailhouse lawyer and aided him in his illegal career.

In recent years Popcorn Sutton continued the fame of the Smokies moonshiner. A native of the Hemphill Bald area of Haywood County, North Carolina, Sutton made moonshine in both his home region and in Cocke County, Tennessee from the 1960s up until he committed suicide on the day before he was to report to a federal prison in 2009. Sutton became the star of several widely distributed documentaries in the 2000s, including *The Last One*. The film follows the bearded, overall-wearing, foul-mouthed Sutton driving around the Smokies in his Model-A Ford truck looking for a place to site a still and then constructing a still where he would make "his last damn run" of illegal liquor. He was later featured in the first season of the reality show *Moonshiners* on the Discovery Channel.

Before the Smokies became a national park, moonshine stills could be found in almost every section of the mountains. Some sections, however, became especially famous, or infamous, for their

A typical moonshine still—located in the woods for privacy, near a running stream or spring

'shine. Historian Durwood Dunn writes about the Chestnut Flats section of Cades Cove which was notorious for moonshining and other illegal activities. Eagle Creek (the stomping grounds of Quill Rose) and Cataloochee also became well-known havens for moonshiners. The Cosby area on the northeastern end of the Park is the section of the Smokies most associated with the illegal liquor business. Author Joseph Earl Dabney named Cocke County as one of four "moonshine capitals of the world" and cited Cosby as its capital.

While the production of illegal corn liquor has continued (and even increased due to the publicity surrounding Popcorn Sutton and other reality show moonshiners), a "legal moonshine" industry centered in Gatlinburg has grown exponentially since the early 2000s. The Old Smoky Distillery pioneered this modern enterprise and attracts hundreds of thousands of visitors to its tasting room on the Gatlinburg strip each year. In the aftermath of Old Smoky's success, at least a half-dozen other distilleries have cropped up in the Smokies region including brands featuring moonshiners Popcorn Sutton and Jim Tom Hedrick.

Indeed, despite Sutton's contention that he was "the last one," moonshine is still very much alive and well in the Great Smoky Mountains.

Editor's Note: You can learn more about the fascinating history of moonshine in Daniel S. Pierce's book *Corn from a Jar: Moonshining in the Great Smoky Mountains.*

Law enforcement officers preparing to destroy a still

GREAT SMOKY
MOUNTAINS
NATIONAL PARK

Mount Cammerer Tower

Photo by Open Parks Network

THE MOUNT CAMMERER

Lookout Tower, built in 1937, stands in dramatic testimony to the legacy of the Depression-era Civilian Conservation Corps in Great Smoky Mountains National Park. The tower crowns the last high peak of the state-line divide on the eastern end of the Park. At this point, the ridge plunges steeply down to the Pigeon River. Using local rock and timber, CCC enrollees built the tower as both a scenic lookout and as a fire tower which was staffed by a fire warden until the 1960s.

The CCC was established in 1933 as a key component of President Franklin Roosevelt's New Deal program. The Corps enrolled 18 - 25 year old men, placed them in camps operated by military personnel, and put them to work in national parks, state parks, and national forests. Enrollees, drawn from a demographic with the highest unemployment rate and the highest likelihood of misbehavior, received room and board, educational and recreation opportunities, and $30 a month,

$25 of which was sent home to their families. In exchange, they worked to restore landscapes damaged by erosion and destructive logging practices and built roads, hiking trails, campgrounds, picnic areas, and other facilities in the nation's public parks and forests. FDR referred to the CCC as his "tree army" in recognition of the millions of tree seedlings planted all over the country.

The first camps came to the Smokies not long after Roosevelt signed the CCC bill into law in 1933. In nine years, tens of thousands of young men in 22 different camps helped transform Great Smoky Mountains National Park. Enrollees left behind many important legacies during that period. CCC crews routed, cleared, smoothed, and in some places blasted rock to create some of the most important hiking trails in the Smokies including Alum Cave, Bull Head, Sugarland Mountain, and parts of the Appalachian Trail. They constructed several beautiful and architecturally

significant buildings for Park administration including the Oconaluftee Ranger Station and the Park Headquarters at Sugarlands. Drive through the Park and you will see stone retaining walls and bridges built skillfully and artistically by the CCC along the roadways. The massive stone platform at the northern end of the Newfound Gap parking lot where FDR dedicated the Park in 1940, and where Dolly Parton helped rededicate it in 2009, was built by enrollees. The remains of CCC camps scattered throughout the Park can still be seen, most visibly along Old Sugarlands Trail near the Sugarlands Visitor Center and Kephart Prong Trail in North Carolina off Newfound Gap Road.

The Mount Cammerer tower attests to the skill and hard work of the Smokies CCC boys. These young men had to haul tools and materials over five miles, gaining over 2,500 feet in elevation, and then cut down trees and quarry rock from the mountainside to build the tower. After completion, the structure served not only as a spectacular lookout point for hikers, but as a fire tower. In the 1960s, the Park Service discontinued its use as a fire tower and the site fell into disrepair. In 1996, Friends of the Smokies funded the restoration of the tower to its original condition and it still rewards visitors who take the challenging trail with some of the best views in the Park and memorializes the stellar work of the CCC.

EXTRAS

HIKING HINT: Reaching the Tower will require a steep, strenuous hike no matter what. You must take either Low Gap Trail (2.1 miles) or Davenport Gap (5.1 miles) to reach the Appalachian Trail junction prior to your scramble to the peak.

FUN FACT: On a clear day, the 360° views from the Tower are nothing short of stunning. From here you can peer into the Tennessee Valley and count the mountain peaks rolling across the horizon.

Look for the **BROAD-WINGED HAWK**

<MOUNT CAMMERER TOWER 18" x 24" Poster art created in 2017 by Michael Korfhage & Joel Anderson

Big Creek

Photos by Joel Anderson

THE BIG CREEK AREA of the Smokies provides almost all of the features treasured by visitors to the Park: picnicking, car and backcountry camping, and hiking trails suitable for all ages and levels of fitness in an environment replete with spectacular mountain streams, old-growth forests, and sweeping mountain views. Despite its close proximity to Interstate 40, the Big Creek entrance is one of the least used in the Park. On most days this is a great place to escape the crowds and enjoy a true wilderness experience.

Big Creek Trail starts near the picnic and campground area. Due to its width, easy grade, and relative smoothness, it makes for a great trail for children. The trail originally was the route of a railroad built by Crestmont Lumber Co. who logged the area in the early years of the 20th century. Visitors can still see evidence of the blasting done by Crestmont crews to carve the railroad grade through solid rock. A little over one mile up the trail, hikers come to Midnight Hole, a large and deep pool in Big Creek framed by huge rocks and a six-foot waterfall. This is a great place to sit quietly and look for trout swimming in the clear water, although it does attract a lot of visitors on summer weekends. Not far above Midnight Hole, Mouse Creek Falls cascades down the mountain, through the trees, and into Big Creek, providing another memorable view. The trail continues to follow the Creek up to Walnut Bottom, the site of a Crestmont logging camp and one of the best spots for backcountry camping in the Smokies.

Another wonderful hike in the Big Creek area is up the beautiful but strenuous Baxter Creek Trail. The trail begins at the picnic area and crosses over Big Creek on a high bridge. The lower end of the trail traverses a huge boulder field and the damp environment makes this area rich with mosses and ferns. The boulders prevented Crestmont from logging here so it also is one of the most accessible areas of old-growth in the Park with some of its largest tuliptrees, cucumber trees, northern red oaks, and silverbells. Above the boulder field, the trail climbs the slopes of Mount Sterling, gaining 4,200 feet in elevation in a little over six miles with scenic vistas of the nearby mountains along the way. At the top, the weary hiker comes to another prime backcountry campsite and the Mount Sterling fire tower. Although the tower is no longer in use, visitors can climb the stairs to the top for panoramic views of the Smokies and nearby Pisgah and Cherokee National Forests.

E X T R A S

HIKING HINT:
This often overlooked trail is one of the easiest in the Park to drive to. Take exit 451 (Waterville Road) off I-40 and immediately turn right. Follow the gravel road to the campground and start exploring.

DID YOU KNOW?
Big Creek is a superb spot for catching "specks" (brook trout). To snag this elusive fish, you'll need to climb through Big Creek's rugged, rhododendron-heavy backcountry. Bring your hiking boots and lots of extra flies.

Look for
BROOK TROUT

BIG CREEK 18" x 24" Poster art created in 2017 by Aaron Johnson & Joel Anderson >

Great
SMOKY MOUNTAINS
BIG CREEK • MIDNIGHT HOLE

Removal

LOVERS of Great Smoky Mountains National Park should never forget that its establishment involved significant personal sacrifice by thousands of individuals. Wealthy industrialists, blue-collar workers, and even school children contributed hard-earned cash and the tax-payers of Tennessee and North Carolina financed $4 million to purchase land for the Park. Philanthropist John D. Rockefeller, Jr. donated $5 million alone to help make what seemed like a delusional dream become a

wonderful reality. However, the most significant sacrifice came from the thousands of farm families whose land was condemned and who were forced to give up their homes, businesses, and churches and leave the Smokies.

When the Park movement began, boosters and politicians promised folks living within the boundaries of the proposed park that they would not lose their land. Tennessee Governor Austin Peay assured a crowd gathered at Elkmont in 1926 that their homes were safe from condemnation, asserting that such an action "would be a blot upon the states that the barbarism of the Huns could not match." But as the national park movement progressed it became apparent that the people of Cades Cove, Walker Valley, the Sugarlands, Greenbrier, Big Creek, Cataloochee, Oconaluftee, and Deep Creek would all have to sell to the North Carolina and Tennessee Park Commissions. Granted the power of eminent domain by their state legislatures, these commissions

forced the residents to pack up whatever they could take and move out.

While some families willingly sold, many others determined to dig in their heels and fight removal. In the late 1920s, someone posted a sign in Cades Cove directed at Chairman of the Tennessee Park Commission David Chapman and Commission land buyers:

> *Col. Chapman You and Hoast*
> *Are Notfy Let the Cove*
> *Peopl Alone Get Out Get*
> *Gone 40M Limit.*

One resident of the Cove wrote to Knoxville newspapers building on Gov. Peay's World War I theme and questioning, "Our ancestors fought in the American Revolution. Have we no right to life, liberty, HOME and happiness? Fresh warm blood from Cades Cove redeemed the soil of France to make the world safe for Democracy - must Cades Cove submit to Kaiserism?" Other residents petitioned John D. Rockefeller, Jr. to step in and pressure the government to allow Smokies residents to stay on their land.

John Oliver of Cades Cove challenged the right of the state to condemn his land in court. The case stretched out over three years with five separate court appearances including two appeals before the Tennessee Supreme Court. Mack Hannah of Cataloochee did the same thing in North Carolina. Both lost their cases.

By the late 1920s and early 1930s, the sight of families packing up their belongings and moving their worldly goods out of the Park area became common. Because of Depression Era economic conditions, the National Park Service did grant annual leases to some families that allowed them to remain on their land. But lease rules limited the ways they could use that land and prohibited cutting timber, digging herbs and roots, building new structures, grazing animals, hunting or manufacturing, selling, or possessing alcohol. One resident complained: "They tell me I can't break a twig, nor pull a flower, after there's a Park. Nor

can I fish with bait for trout, nor kill a boomer (red squirrel) nor bear on land owned by my pap and grandpap and his pap before him."

Most families took advantage of the leases as a temporary measure, but some stayed for the rest of their lives. The five Walker sisters, who remained in their cabin in Little Greenbrier until the last one died in 1964, became a popular tourist attraction and sold their handicrafts to visitors. The famous sisters were even profiled in Saturday Evening Post in 1946.

Removal was a wrenching experience for many Smokies families. As Ranger Glen Cardwell, whose family had to leave Greenbrier, recalled, "You can buy a farm anywhere, but tearing up your community does something to your spirit." All Glen's father wanted for his birthday in his later years was to be driven back into Greenbrier to revisit and reminisce about the grown-over sites where he and his family and friends had lived, worked, worshipped, and played. Louisa Walker penned a short poem expressing the sadness she and her sisters felt at the loss of their beloved community:

But now the park commissioners
Comes all dressed in clothes so gay
Saying this old mountain home of yours
We must now take away.

Many of these lost communities still hold reunions to this day.

As people moved out, the Park Service began dismantling or burning down most of the homes, barns, and outbuildings. Some of the homes were sturdy, modern structures built with fine timber.

Woody House, Cataloochee

A farmer's gravesite

Beech Grove School, Cataloochee

These were sold, dismantled and the materials used to build new homes outside the Park. Duane Oliver's family took apart a home in the Proctor section of Hazel Creek and built a home in Hazelwood in the next county. Less sturdy structures were burned down by Park Service employees who argued that folks were using the abandoned homes and barns "for moonshining and other immoral purposes." For many former residents the demolition of their communities proved to be the final insult. As historian, and John Oliver's grandson, Durwood Dunn observed: "Having destroyed the community of Cades Cove by eminent domain, the community's corpse was now to be mutilated beyond recognition."

In the early 1940s, communities on Noland, Forney, Hazel, and Eagle Creeks also experienced the pain of removal. The Tennessee Valley Authority condemned their land when the Fontana Dam flooded part of the North Shore of the Little Tennessee River and cut off road access to the area.

For years, many families removed from the area remained bitter about this sad episode. The Park Service often did not help the situation with an interpretive framework that sugarcoated removal and downplayed any controversy. However, under the leadership of Superintendent Dale Ditmanson (2004-2013), the Park Service consciously recognized the sacrifice and pain of the removal experience. During the celebration of the Park's 75th birthday, Ditmanson and other Park staff visited all of the surrounding communities and publicly thanked the families of those removed and acknowledged their sacrifice. At the rededication of the Park before a crowd of dignitaries at Newfound Gap, individuals born and raised in Cataloochee, Cades Cove, Greenbrier, Sugarlands, and other Smokies communities were provided seats of honor in the front of the public seating and Ditmanson once again publicly recognized their sacrifice. The museum at the Oconaluftee Visitors Center, opened in 2011, also does a much better job of realistically depicting mountain life and the issue of removal.

Visitors to the Park can still see evidence of the lives of the people removed from the Smokies today. The Park Service has preserved numerous churches, barns, and homes, most notably in Cades Cove and Cataloochee, and visitors who look closely can see the foundations, chimneys, and rock walls left behind. Most tellingly, over 150 cemeteries maintained by the Park Service are also scattered throughout the Smokies, their headstones standing in silent memorial to the sacrifice paid by poor farmers to provide land for the most visited national park in the United States.

Barn in Cataloochee

Cades Cove Primitive Baptist Church

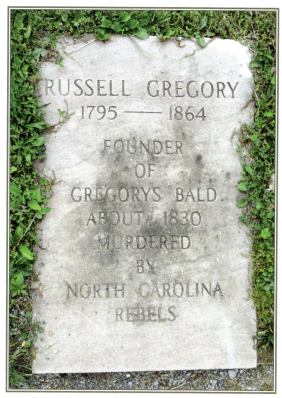

Grave of Cades Cove Patriarch Russell Gregory

"In the peaceful cemetery of the old Primitive Baptist Church lie the first and last John Oliver – the founding settler and his great-grandson – some sixty feet apart. Within these four generations of Olivers the community of Cades Cove was born, flourished for a season, and died. Nothing can rob them now of their beloved cove or cherished community . . . With the passage of time, the collective consciousness of their community has dimmed to extinction, but among their descendants its afterglow still illumines Cades Cove." — Historian Durwood Dunn, author of *Cades Cove: The Life* and *Death of a Southern Appalachian Community*

Caldwell House, Cataloochee

CATALOOCHEE

GREAT SMOKY MOUNTAINS NATIONAL PARK

Elk

Photos by Joel Anderson

ONE UNFORGETTABLE

sensory experience in Cataloochee or Oconaluftee is to see and hear a 700+ pound bull elk lift its head and issue a piercingly eerie bugle that echoes off the mountainsides. Such sights and sounds had been absent from the Smokies since the late 1700s as elk were extirpated from the area due to overhunting.

That changed in the early 2000s when Park Service officials committed to reintroducing wildlife that had once lived in the Smokies. They teamed up with local members of the Rocky Mountain Elk Foundation, Friends of the Smokies, the Great Smoky Mountains Association, and the University of Tennessee to bring elk back to the region. In 2001, an initial herd of 25 animals were transported from Land Between the Lakes National Recreation Area on the border of Tennessee and Kentucky to Cataloochee. Officials brought an additional 27 elk

from Canada in 2002. Wildlife biologists in the Park tagged all the animals and placed radio transmitters around their necks to monitor the herd.

Since those initial reintroductions, the herd has grown to over 150 and elk have migrated into the Oconaluftee area near the visitors center and even into areas outside the Park. One wandering young bull elk from the Smokies was spotted almost 100 miles away in Pickens County, South Carolina in the fall of 2016. In the future, elk will spread further into the Park, perhaps as far as the prime habitat of Cades Cove.

The elk can be seen year round in the meadows near the Oconaluftee Visitor Center along Newfound Gap Road and in Cataloochee. As a result, visitation to the Cataloochee section has exploded since 2001 despite visitors having to negotiate eleven miles of steep, winding roads with no guard rails (five miles of which are

unpaved) to get to the valley. The elk put on an especially memorable show during the fall mating season when the bulls spar for control of harems of females and their distinctive bugles reverberate through the valley as they warn competitors away.

While the elk may look gentle, even tame, they can be extremely dangerous. These are huge, powerful animals. Many of the bulls have massive, sharply-pointed antlers and all elk have sharp hooves that they use for self-defense. Approaching elk is not only dangerous but can be expensive as well. The National Park Service reminds visitors that, "Willfully approaching within 50 yards (150 feet), or any distance that disturbs or displaces elk, is illegal in the park" and can result in "fines or arrest." Visitors who encounter an elk on a trail should quietly step off the path, get behind a tree or rock and allow the animal to pass.

During peak visitation periods the volunteer "Elk Bugle Corps" helps to monitor interactions between visitors and elk and educate the public about the reintroduction program and elk behavior.

Elk scat

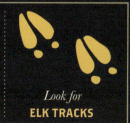
<CATALOOCHEE ELK 18" x 24" Poster art created in 2017 by Aaron Johnson & Joel Anderson

Great Smoky Mountains
NATIONAL PARK

Palmer Chapel

BUILT IN 1898, Palmer Chapel Methodist is a picturesque little church located on the banks of Cataloochee Creek. Evangelical Christianity was very important to the European settlers who came to the Great Smoky Mountains and most larger communities had at least one church. Protestant groups predominated; there was not a great deal of variety in terms of denominational choices in the Smokies. As Florence Cope Bush put it, "There were folk who were Methodist, Holiness, Missionary Baptist, Primitive Baptist, footwashing Baptist, a sprinkling of Presbyterians, and a few Campbellites (Church of Christ)."

Most of the church buildings in the Smokies, like Palmer Chapel, were of the white clapboard variety, but churches met in all kinds of spaces including schools and community buildings. At the Little River Lumber Co. camp at Tremont, church met in the community center, a building that also served as school, movie theater, and sometime wrestling arena. Little River manager D.L. "Doc" Tipton referred to it as a "house of education, salvation, hellfire and damnation" as some folks in the region frowned on movies as sinful.

Although there were denominational differences, services in most of these churches were similar, featuring informal and spontaneous worship, energetic preaching, and congregations that participated actively in the service. In his novel *Cataloochee*, Wayne Caldwell describes a typical preacher in the area where being "called" by God to preach was more important than theological education: "In those forty years (of his ministry) he preached from a head full of Bible and a heart primed by conviction. To write out a sermon would not have occurred to him, nor would notes have been welcome before him. He liked the Spirit to urge him first one way, then another, so his sermons bounded through both testaments like bunches of jumped jackrabbits." Because of the expense of pianos and the association of banjoes and fiddles with the "devil's music," singing was generally a capella using the old Southern Harmony shaped-note songbooks.

Churches in the region did more than provide for the religious needs of these communities. They also served as community hubs, hosts of dinners on the grounds, baptisms, lodge meetings, women's organizations, summer revivals, and community singing conventions. Summer revivals were especially important events in the Smokies and nearly everyone, saved or unsaved, came together for up to two weeks in late summer when the "crops were laid by" and needed little tending until the harvest. Folks flocked to revivals not only for the preaching and singing, but to catch up on the latest community news, court a beau, and some even to drink, fight, carouse, and compete with the preachers for converts.

Palmer Chapel Methodist and other churches in the Smokies played an important part in the story of community removal. It was from the pulpit in Palmer Chapel that preacher Pat Davis announced to a stunned and angry Cataloochee community that their land was going to be part of Great Smoky Mountains National Park and they were going to have to move away. Today, the church hosts an annual reunion of folks related to the former inhabitants of the area, complete with a worship service which always features the singing of "Shall We Gather at the River" and a dinner on the ground in the churchyard.

Photos by Joel Anderson

<PALMER CHAPEL Poster art based on a 30" x 40" acrylic painting created in 2017 by Joel Anderson

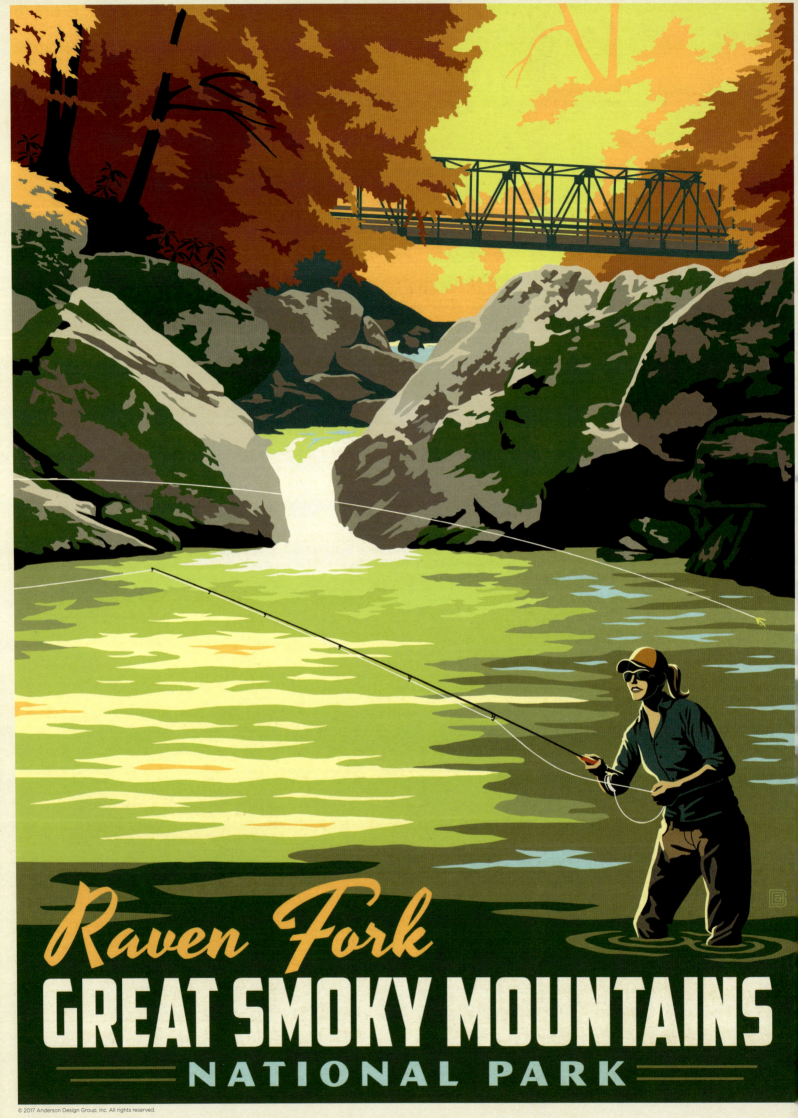

Raven Fork
GREAT SMOKY MOUNTAINS
NATIONAL PARK

Raven Fork

AWE-INSPIRING, rugged, wild, remote, painful, dangerous, and serene are all adjectives that come to mind with a visit into the Raven Fork Gorge. If you want a trip into the heart of a true wilderness then this is the place for you, but you have to work for the privilege. That work, however, will be rewarded with a unique and humbling experience in a place where, in the words of the 1964 Wilderness Act, "the earth and its community of life are untrammeled by man, where man himself is a visitor who does not remain."

The easiest way to access the area is to take Big Cove Road out of Cherokee, NC until you reach the Cherokee fish hatchery. Straight Fork Road begins on the left side of the hatchery (although it looks like it might be a driveway) and continues as a dirt road into the Park. After approximately three miles you'll see a sign for the beginning of Hyatt Ridge Trail and a small parking area on the left.

The hike into Raven Fork begins with a steep two-mile climb up the trail to Hyatt Ridge alongside a cascading mountain stream on your left. The trail tops out on Hyatt Ridge and then descends toward Raven Fork on Enloe Creek Trail. This trail is part of the 300-mile Benton MacKaye Trail that runs from Springer Mountain, Georgia (the southern terminus of the Appalachian Trail) to Davenport Gap on the Tennessee-North Carolina line on the eastern edge of the Park.

Once you cross Hyatt Ridge, you have entered a unique Smoky Mountain rain forest environment. Due to its remote location, the Raven Fork Gorge experienced limited logging activity. Hiking down Enloe Creek Trail, you pass through one of the most lush and diverse old-growth forests in the Park with large maple, beech, cherry, hickory, and yellow buckeye trees lining the way. Notice the masses of epiphytic mosses and ferns growing on boulders and large branches of beech trees near the bottom of the Gorge. Sometimes referred to as "air plants," epiphytes get their nutrients and moisture from the air, from rainfall, and from plant debris that accumulates on rock and tree branch surfaces.

After one mile on Enloe Creek Trail, the hiker arrives at an iron bridge, the only access to Raven Fork on a marked trail. The view up and down Raven Fork from this bridge is one of the most spectacular in the Park as the scene is framed by massive boulders, a resplendent plant environment, and roaring waterfalls that plummet into deep pools. The noise of the rushing waters is almost overwhelming. Indeed, you begin to hear Raven Fork almost half-a-mile before you get to it.

The Enloe Creek Backcountry Campsite is just across the bridge and offers one of the most beautiful camp settings anywhere. The boulders above the campsite are also a wonderful place to set up a hammock for an afternoon nap.

Entry to Raven Fork up or down stream from the bridge requires considerable rock hopping. Anyone who attempts this should proceed with caution. It is much easier to move about when water levels are low and you can walk in the stream. Cautious effort, however, will be rewarded with a seemingly unending procession of gorgeous waterfalls and plunge pools in both directions. These pools also teem with speckled trout. It is an unforgettable experience to catch one of these beauties in such an epic setting.

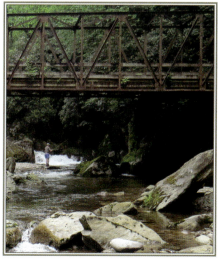

Photos by Joel Anderson

<RAVEN FORK 18" x 24" Poster created in 2017 by Aaron Johnson & Joel Anderson

Speckled Trout

"JEWEL-LIKE and nearly iridescent, a treasure only nature could produce," is how journalist Gary Garth described the southern Brook Trout. Commonly known in the region as native trout, speckled trout, or "specks," they are the only native trout in the Smokies. Although small in comparison to other trout, fly fishermen come to the Smokies for the thrill of landing this wild, aggressive fish displaying almost fluorescent flashes of red and orange on its underside.

Due to logging, acidification of streams due to air pollution, and the introduction of non-native trout, speckled trout have lost much of their range in the region. The introduction of brown and rainbow trout into Smokies streams in the early part of the 20th century has had an especially devastating impact on native fish.

Browns and rainbows grow much larger and faster than brook trout, produce more young, compete for food resources, and feed on young "specks." As a result, by the 1980s the native trout were forced out of much of their traditional range and increasingly found in isolated populations in the headwaters of streams above 3,000 feet. In 1976, populations of brook trout had dropped so low that the Park Service banned fishermen from harvesting the fish.

Ten years later, Park fisheries biologists initiated a new program to restore brook trout populations in the Park. Using natural barriers such as waterfalls and cascades, staff and volunteers removed the brown and rainbow trout from above the barrier to create a stream environment where brook trout could thrive and reproduce effectively. These efforts

have helped to restore speckled trout populations and now the fish inhabit over 130 miles of the Park's 800 miles of fishable streams. Indeed, populations have recovered enough so that fishermen can now keep up to five brook trout that are over seven inches long per day.

It is fitting that the strikingly colored brook trout are usually found in stunning locations. They tend to hide in the headwaters of most of the larger streams on both sides of the Smokies, especially above waterfalls. Fishing for brook trout often involves scrambling over rocks, crawling through rhododendron, and a stealthy approach to a plunge pool as these wild trout spook easily. However, catching a "speck" in the beautiful environs of Raven Fork, Lynn Camp Prong, or the headwaters of Hazel, Forney, or Big Creeks is an experience even the most seasoned fisherman will not soon forget.

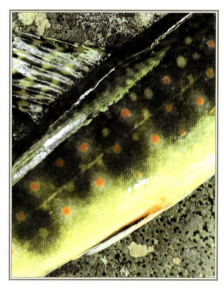

Photos by Joel Anderson

EXTRAS

★ FUN FACT:
Despite a wide variety, aquatic insect populations remain low in the Park. This meager food supply prevents most specks from ever growing larger than 8 inches or living longer than 4 years.

ⓘ DID YOU KNOW?
Brook trout enjoy rapidly flowing streams strewn with boulders (which are easy to dart behind). The Little River's Middle Prong is a congenial spot.

Look for the
NORTHERN WATER SNAKE

SPECKLED TROUT 18" x 24" Poster art created in 2017 by Derek Anderson & Joel Anderson

Backcountry Camping   Campsite   Fly Fishing

APPALACHIAN TRAIL

JENKINS RIDGE TRAIL

HAZEL CREEK TRAIL

28 Backcountry Camping

29 Horseback Riding

EAGLE CREEK

26 Fly Fishing

LOST COVE TRAIL

28 Backcountry Camping

28 Backcountry Camping

HAZEL CREEK

FORNEY CREEK

NOLAND CREEK TRAIL

29 Horseback Riding

26 Fly Fishing

DEEP CREEK

FONTANA LAKE

29 Horseback Riding

LAKESHORE TRAIL

29 Horseback Riding

28 Backcountry Camping

NOLAND CREEK

27 Car Camping

30 Fontana Lake

PART 4 — *Gateway to Adventure*

The Southwestern Section of the Park (Bryson City to Fontana Dam)

Photo by DepositPhotos.com

The southwest region of the Park, from Deep Creek to Hazel Creek and beyond Fontana Lake on the Park's southern border, is known for both its wild beauty as well as its plethora of opportunities for outdoor recreation. From trout fishing and kayaking to horseback riding, car camping, and backcountry hiking, you can pretty much do it all here. Road access is limited so tourism is light. For anyone seeking a Smoky Mountain getaway without the crowds, the southwest is hard to beat.

Deep, Forney, Noland, Hazel, Eagle, and Twenty-mile Creeks offer some of the best fly fishing for brown, rainbow, and native brook trout in the Eastern U.S. Brown and rainbow trout tend to populate streams that are easily accessible by car. Since water is in no short supply at GSMNP, you're bound to see fishermen pulling on their waders in any of the trailhead parking lots. Unlike their bigger, more sociable cousins however, brook trout live in harder-to-reach stream beds in the backcountry. Be prepared to hike (and carry your gear) over rugged terrain for a chance to

land one of these lustrous treasures.

Fontana Lake offers stunning scenery and a variety of boating opportunities from jet boats to pontoon boats to canoes and kayaks. Spend a day on the Park's largest body of water and explore its many branches and tributaries. Be sure to drive across 480-foot tall Fontana Dam, the tallest dam east of the Mississippi River. Backpack-laden individuals can often be spotted crossing over the top of the dam; the Appalachian Trail runs through here. Twentymile Trail and Lakeshore Trail

both offer leisurely (level) strolls by the water and can be enjoyed on foot or by horseback.

Deep Creek is also an ideal location for a family car camping experience. In addition, this area offers some of the best backcountry camping in the Park and visitors can plan backpacking trips for one night or ten. Just outside the Park boundary, visitors will find world-class whitewater activities on the Nantahala River and mountain biking on the Tsali trail system.

Photo by Joel Anderson

Car Camping

CAR CAMPING, also called Frontcountry Camping, has a long and colorful history in Great Smoky Mountains National Park. The national parks, the Smokies, and the automobile have been inextricably tied together since the 1920s. Local automobile clubs vigorously supported both the expansion of the parks system and the development of roadways within existing national parks. These clubs, along with other booster groups, implanted the "Great American Road Trip" idea (including car camping in a national park) into the psyche of middle-class Americans. Henry Ford himself, along with his fellow "Vagabonds" Thomas Edison and Harvey Firestone, pioneered and publicized the joys of camping in the Smokies in the 1920s.

Indeed, when the Park became a reality, visitors flocked to the Smokies in their cars and started camping on the roadsides in a haphazard fashion, creating both traffic and sanitation problems. Visitors even commandeered abandoned CCC camps and turned them into makeshift campgrounds. In order to address this problem, Park Superintendent Ross Eakin created temporary campgrounds at Deep Creek, Smokemont, Elkmont, and Cades Cove in 1935. Throughout the remainder of the decade, the CCC worked to improve these campgrounds and make them permanent, especially the sanitary facilities, and added new sites.

Today, Great Smoky Mountains National Park has ten developed frontcountry campgrounds with over 900 campsites where individuals and groups may experience the Park in a tent or camper. Smokies campgrounds range from the relatively remote Big Creek Campground on the eastern side of the Park to the largest campground, Elkmont, with 220 sites only a short drive away from Gatlinburg. While trailers and RVs are allowed at some of the larger campgrounds, facilities are decidedly, and intentionally, barebones with only a fire ring and a picnic table; there are no showers, no electric or sewer hookups, and no wi-fi. Those who prefer more amenities can easily find plenty of campgrounds with these services near almost all of the Park entrances, but they won't have the scenery that the Park offers.

Campsites at the four largest campgrounds (Cosby, Cades Cove, Elkmont, and Smokemont) as well as at Cataloochee can be reserved at www.Recreation.gov. Groups larger than eight can also reserve tents-only group campsites at seven sites in the Park. The Cades Cove and Smokemont Campgrounds are open year-round while the others open at various times in the spring and close in late fall.

One of the great pleasures of camping in the Smokies is sitting around the campfire, sharing stories, singing songs, and roasting marshmallows to sandwich between graham crackers and a chocolate bar for s'mores. Because of the devastating impact of invasive species on plant life in the Park, however, the Park Service now requires campers to use only dead and downed wood found on site or commercially heat-treated firewood. Treated wood is available at campground stores at Cades Cove, Elkmont, and Smokemont and at most grocery, hardware, and convenience stores right outside the Park.

Car camping in the Smokies is a way to experience a great American tradition in an unforgettable environment. Park campgrounds offer opportunities for hiking, playing in the streams, relaxing by a campfire, and enjoying the scenery and wildlife in an up-close and personal way. Camping together is also a wonderful way to strengthen the bonds of friendship and family away from the noise, hustle and bustle, and intrusive connectivity of modern life.

<CAR CAMPING 18" x 24" Poster art created in 2017 by Aaron Johnson & Joel Anderson

Deep Creek

GREAT SMOKY

MOUNTAINS NATIONAL PARK

Deep Creek

THE DEEP CREEK entrance to the Park provides a wonderful gateway into the many recreational adventures the Smokies have to offer. The area (right outside of the charming mountain town of Bryson City, North Carolina) has great opportunities for hiking, picnicking, backpacking, car camping, biking, horseback riding, waterfall viewing, fly fishing, and tubing.

When visitors come through the Deep Creek entrance, they are greeted by Deep Creek Campground and a large picnic area. The campground has 92 sites and is open April to November with the picnic area open year round. Deep Creek Trail, which begins just above the picnic area, is open to hikers and horses and provides access to innumerable trails leading deep into the Smokies wilderness. It is also one of the few trails in the park which is accessible for bike riding along the old road grade from its lower end. There are three picturesque waterfalls within a mile of the picnic area: Juney Whank, Tom Branch, and Indian Creek.

While the Park Service discourages this activity, Deep Creek is also very popular for tubing and a number of businesses renting tubes line the road outside the Park entrance. The National Park Service does remind visitors that "serious water-related injuries occur every year in the park and drowning is the second leading cause of death in the park."

Deep Creek is rich in history and

Photo by Joel Anderson

visitors can see the walls, foundations, and crumbling chimneys left behind by the people who once farmed its banks. The area was also the stomping grounds for three legendary residents of the Smokies: Tsali, Horace Kephart and Mark Cathey. Tsali, a Cherokee removal martyr, hid out in 1838 in a rock shelter on the slopes of Clingmans Dome up the left fork of Deep Creek with his family to evade capture by federal troops. He was later captured and executed for killing two soldiers who were trying to remove him from his home and his life is memorialized in the outdoor drama "Unto These Hills." While noted writer and outdoorsman Kephart is most often associated with Hazel Creek, one of his favorite summer campsites was the Bryson Place (now Backcountry Campsite #57) on Deep Creek. After his death, local Boy Scouts placed a millstone at the site with a plaque commemorating the author and his book *Camping and Woodcraft*, the Boy Scout manual of that day. Uncle Mark Cathey was a colorful local character, a legendary hunter with nearly one hundred notches in his bear gun, and a fly fisherman who had the unique ability to "tantalize" trout into striking his lures. He never left the stream empty handed even when others had no luck. Visitors from all over the world came to Deep Creek to fish with him and listen to his homespun wisdom. Cathey is still a legend among trout fishing aficionados.

EXTRAS

HIKING HINT:
Deep Creek is an excellent area for kids and older adults to have an idyllic Smokies experience without having to climb a mountain. The trail is wide and slopes only gently.

TRAVEL TIP:
Deep Creek offers numerous opportunities for trout fishing. One of our favorite spots is at the foot of Tom Branch Falls.

At dusk, look for **RACCOONS**

<DEEP CREEK 18" x 24" Poster art created in 2017 by Derek Anderson & Joel Anderson

Fly Fishing

THE GREAT SMOKY Mountains are a Mecca for fly fishermen with world-renowned streams such as Hazel Creek, Deep Creek, Raven Fork, Cataloochee Creek, Big Creek, the Little Pigeon River, Little River, and Abrams Creek. Anglers flock to the Smokies seeking wild brown and rainbow trout (introduced to the area in the early 20th century) on the lower reaches of these streams and native brook, or speckled, trout at high elevation.

Fly fishing for wild trout in the Smokies is a challenging experience for the angler as the National Park Service no longer stocks the streams with hatchery-raised fish. As a result, the wild trout in the streams here can be extremely skittish. This fact, along with the clarity of the Park's streams, requires the fisherman to use stealth to slowly and carefully approach the area they wish to fish. There are occasions when the fish will feed aggressively as large numbers of insects hatch from their larval stage and emerge from the water, setting off a feeding frenzy. The trout of the Smokies are not particularly large, but they make up for this with their fight, their brilliant colors, and the gorgeous stream settings where they are caught.

Many Smokies streams offer the rare opportunity to achieve a fly fisherman's "Grand Slam" for the eastern U.S., catching a brown, rainbow, and brook trout in the same day, although this can involve considerable hiking and some good luck. Hazel Creek offers the even rarer chance to bag a "Royal Slam" which adds a smallmouth bass or redeye, caught in the cove where Hazel Creek empties into Fontana Lake, to the mix.

Fishing in the Park is allowed year-round and requires either a Tennessee or North Carolina fishing license or permit. Only artificial lures with a single hook may be employed; using bait, live or otherwise, is prohibited. Anglers can keep up to five fish per day but they must be at least seven inches in length.

Fly fishing in Great Smoky Mountains is as much about the experience as it is about catching fish. Indeed, for many committed anglers fishing these mountain streams is a spiritual event. Author Harry Middleton, writing about his fly fishing experiences on Hazel Creek in *On the Spine of Time*, eloquently expresses what brought him back to the Smokies, rod in hand, again and again:

"I come for the beauty and the good fishing rather than grand truths, though these too are here scattered about the creek bottoms like weathered stones. The soft light of dusk, a trout's rise, the sound of nothing but water over stones are glamour and excitement enough. Mountain solitude is deep and wide and abiding and yet coiled tight as a snake, something alive, ready to give way at any instant to something as ordinary as birdsong or as confounding and bewitching as a trout's sudden inexplicable leap out of a stream's cold waters and into the sun's bright warm light."

Photos by Joel Anderson

FLY FISHING 18" x 24" Poster art created in 2017 by Aaron Johnson & Joel Anderson >

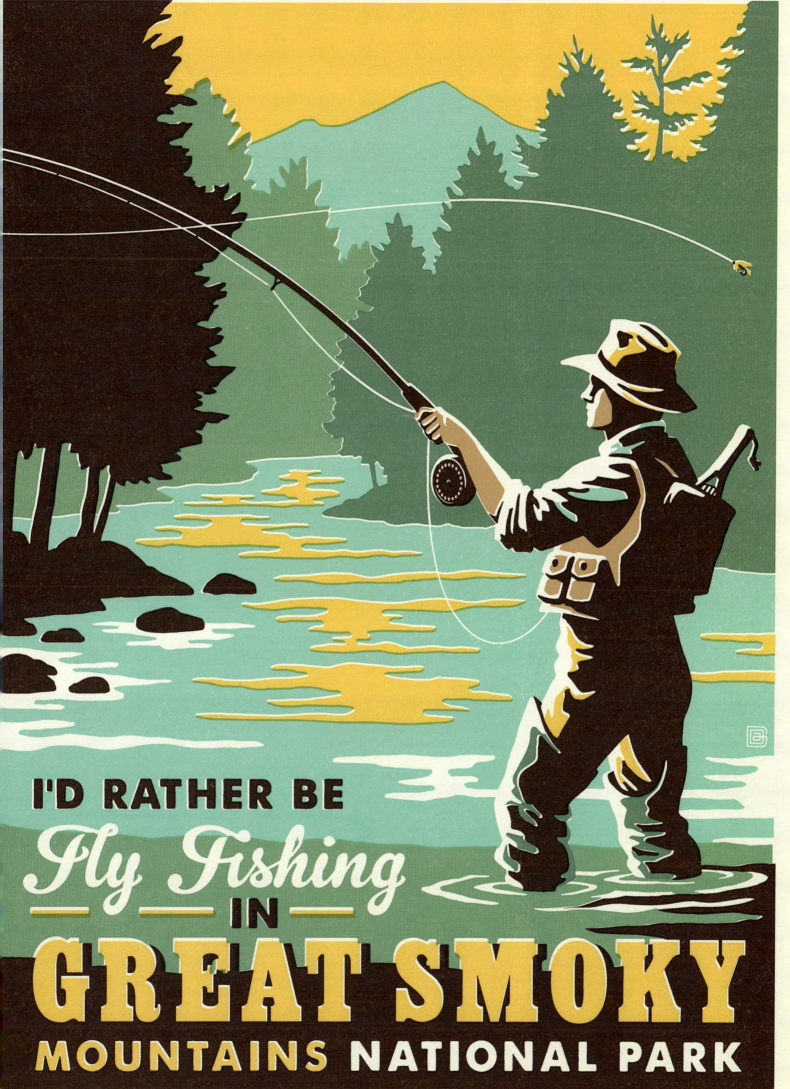

I'D RATHER BE

Fly Fishing

IN

GREAT SMOKY

MOUNTAINS NATIONAL PARK

EXPERIENCE BACKCOUNTRY CAMPING

GREAT SMOKY MOUNTAINS
NATIONAL PARK

Backcountry Camping

FOR THOSE WILLING and able, the best way to experience the Great Smoky Mountains is to strap on a backpack, hike into the backcountry, and spend a few nights in the wilderness. With over 80 designated backcountry campsites and 15 trail shelters, Great Smoky Mountains National Park is an ideal place for both novice and experienced backpackers. Those eager for a Smokies experience away from the crowds can choose from a wide variety of campsites scattered throughout the Park, most along streams or at high elevation.

Hikes into backcountry campsites can vary from short in-and-out walks of a few miles along relatively level railroad grades, to weeks-long adventure treks requiring lung-busting climbs and scrambles through dense vegetation. One of the most popular backpacking trips in the Park, but not one for the novice, is the 71.6 mile trip on the Smokies sec-tion of the Appalachian Trail. Shorter, flatter hikes to backcountry sites along Big, Cataloochee, Deep, Noland, Hazel, or Abrams Creeks are a good way to introduce novices and children to the pleasures of backpacking. Those who want a wilderness experience but prefer a steak to a freeze-dried meal, might try Hazel Creek where campers use make-shift aluminum carts with bicycle wheels (known as "Hazel Creek Buggies" or "Hazel Creek Cadillacs") to pack in large coolers, big tents, and cots.

For safety reasons, backcountry campers must register with Park authorities, pay a small camping fee, and only camp at designated sites. All sites include cable systems to keep food and "odorous" items, like toothpaste, away from bears and other hungry critters.

The Smokies have a long tradition of backpacking. Many of the early advocates for the national park were intrepid backpackers and left vivid records of their experiences. Horace Kephart wrote *Our Southern Highlanders* and the bible of early backpacking aficionados, *Camping and Woodcraft,* based on his many backcountry experiences in the Smokies. Kephart's good friend Paul Fink wrote one of the first accounts of a wilderness experience in the Smokies (*Backpacking was the Only Way*), and their mutual friend photographer, George Masa, often documented their trips on film.

One of the most eloquent of these early backpackers was Harvey Broome, a Knoxville lawyer, a founder of the Wilderness Society, and author of *Out Under the Sky of the Great Smokies*, a compilation of his hiking and backpacking journals over more than fifty years. Broome penned one of the best reasons for backpacking in this book: "Wilderness is vastly different from the clutter and clatter of much of our civilized world. In wilderness one experiences exhilaration and joy. In its freedom and simplicity, in its vitality and immense variety, happiness may not only be pursued; it is ofttimes found."

Photos by Joel Anderson

<BACKCOUNTRY CAMPING 18" x 24" Poster art created in 2017 by Michael Korfhage & Joel Anderson

GREAT SMOKY MOUNTAINS
NATIONAL PARK

Horseback Riding

Great Smoky Mountains National Park Archives

Photo by Allison Bailey

HORSES have played an integral role in the history of Great Smoky Mountains National Park since the first white traders and settlers arrived in the region, bringing their animals with them. Horses were traditionally used in the region as draft animals, for plowing fields and pulling wagons and sleds. However, since the early years of the 20th century, trail riding in the Smokies has been a popular feature of many visitors' experience. Early national park boosters often took influential visitors into the backcountry on horseback. Today the Park is a virtual paradise for horseback riding and approximately 550 miles of trails scattered throughout the Park are open for riding.

Seeing the Park from the back of a horse is an experience available to those who have never ridden before and for horse owners with long experience. Concessionaires operate stables open to the public (two near Gatlinburg, one in Cades Cove, and one at Smokemont) and offer guided trail rides, hayrides, and carriage and wagon rides. These stables are open from mid-March through late November and provide rides from forty-five-minutes to several hours in length. Guides lead groups of riders into the backcountry, through stately forests, alongside mountain streams, and to scenic views.

Visitors can also bring their own horses to the Park and take them on any of the designated horse trails. Trails open to horses are marked by dotted lines on the Park trail map. Many campsites are also open for horseback riders as well and riders can plan expeditions lasting over several days to explore some of the most scenic areas of the Smokies, fish the streams, and enjoy the solitude interrupted only by the clip-clop of their horses' hooves. The Park also maintains five drive-in horse camps at Cades Cove, Cataloochee, Big Creek, Round Bottom, and Towstring.

In order to minimize the environmental impact of such a large animal in the Smokies, the Park has a number of important rules horseback riders need to follow. Horses must be tied up at hitchracks or, where these are not available, cross-tied so that they cannot damage trees and other vegetation. Riders should always stay on designated trails, keep their horses in single file in the center of the trail, and, in order to prevent erosion, avoid trails that are extremely muddy, frozen, or thawing.

Trails range in difficulty from beginner to experienced and the latter can be a challenge for even the most experienced horse and rider. While some trails follow old road beds, many horse trails cross streams or are very steep, narrow, and rocky. Remoteness and difficulty of access often make trail maintenance a challenge and riders may encounter rugged conditions along some trails. Check for trail conditions or closures prior to beginning your trip and report downed trees or landslides to a ranger if encountered while on the trail. Interested visitors should consult the Park's website for complete information.

EXTRAS

⭐ **TRAIL TIP:**
Take Deep Creek Horse Trail for an uphill adventure. Crossing over Noland Divide, the trail ends in the high mountain country on Clingmans Dome Road!

ℹ **DID YOU KNOW?**
The Park's southernmost border area features a horse-friendly Lakeshore Trail with lovely views of Fontana Lake.

Look for
WILD TURKEY

<HORSEBACK RIDING Poster art based on a 27" x 36" oil painting created in 2017 by Kai Carpenter

FONTANA LAKE

Great
SMOKY MOUNTAINS
NATIONAL PARK

© 2017 Anderson Design Group, Inc. All rights reserved.

Fontana Lake

Photo by Joel Anderson

MUCH OF THE southwest border of Great Smoky Mountains National Park is formed by Fontana Lake which provides a spectacular foreground for the mountains. The 17-mile long lake stretches from just outside Bryson City, North Carolina to the Fontana Dam located west of the lake's confluence with Eagle Creek. It is deep and relatively narrow, with numerous picturesque islands and long coves where crystal-clear mountain streams enter the lake.

Fontana Lake was created in 1944 when the Tennessee Valley Authority completed the 480-foot Fontana Dam, the highest dam in the eastern United States, impounding the waters of the Little Tennessee River. The dam was a wartime project to provide electricity to the Alcoa Aluminum plant in East Tennessee which produced massive amounts of aluminum for the war effort, and for the top-secret effort in Oak Ridge to build an atomic bomb.

The dizzying urgency of the project led to an unprecedented construction schedule and involved the importation of thousands of workers to the remote area. TVA workers poured the first concrete in January 1942 and closed the spillways in November 1944, completing the dam in less than three years.

Sadly, the flooding of the valley cut off the only road to Fontana's North Shore and the communities clustered around Noland, Forney, Hazel, and Eagle Creeks. The flooding forced a second major removal of families from the Smokies when TVA condemned the land and turned it over to the National Park Service for inclusion in the Park. Once again the sights of families loading up their belongings and moving out of the area became common.

Despite its controversial history, the Fontana Lake area provides some of the best recreational opportunities in the Smokies. Trails beginning at Fontana Dam (the Appalachian Trail crosses the dam) and along Lakeshore Road take hikers, backpackers, fishermen, and horseback riders into the North Shore area, one of the most remote sections of the Park. Here visitors can experience both the wilderness of the Smokies and the rich history of a landscape that was inhabited up until the mid-1940s. Scattered foundations and chimneys, evidences of copper mining, dilapidated remains of logging equipment, and even the rusty hulks of old cars serve as reminders of the communities that once thrived here. Visitors can avoid a long hike into Hazel Creek and take a boat shuttle from the Fontana Marina to the site of the logging town of Proctor, the Hazel Creek Trail, and the fishing and backpacking hub of Hazel Creek itself.

On the lake visitors enjoy water skiing, pontoon boat or jet boat excursions, or peaceful paddles in canoes or kayaks around the lake's many secluded coves. Boats and equipment can be rented from vendors at the many Fontana marinas. The Nantahala National Forest covers much of the south side of the Lake and is especially famous for the world-class Tsali system of mountain bike trails which offer winding lakeside rides appropriate for most skill levels and spectacular views of the Smokies across the Lake. The Nantahala River, one of the most popular whitewater rivers in the Southeast U.S., also flows into Fontana Lake and provides a wide variety of whitewater adventures.

EXTRAS

★ TRAVEL TIP:
Lake Fontana has a shoreline of about 240 miles. Take a kayak or canoe and explore the lake's many coves, streams and branches that snake around the Smoky Mountains.

ⓘ DID YOU KNOW?
For a lake, Fontana has surprisingly clear water. You can often see rocks and fish 20+ feet below the surface!

Look (and listen) for the
AMERICAN BULLFROG

<FONTANA LAKE 18" x 24" Poster art created in 2017 by Derek Anderson & Joel Anderson

Great Smoky MOUNTAINS

AMERICA'S MOST VISITED **NATIONAL PARK**

Animal and Plant Life

Barred Owl

Black-chinned Red Salamander

ON A HOT SUMMER DAY, humans may seem like the most prevalent species in Great Smoky Mountains National Park. With over 10 million visitors a year, the Smokies are no doubt a teeming hive for nature-loving tourists. And yet, despite the traffic and packed parking lots, this 800 square mile mountain paradise hosts an enormous diversity of plants and wildlife. Over 19,000 species of living organisms have been documented in the Park thus far. And experts say there is plenty more yet to be found.

Of what we know, there are at least 100 varying types of trees, 1,500 different wildflowers, 200 birds, 68 mammals, 43 amphibians, 39 reptiles, 67 fish, and lots and lots of ferns, moss, and mushrooms. How is such variety possible? Several factors come into play, but the most obvious are the temperate climate, abundant rainfall, and the elevation range (from 850 - 6,643 feet). You'd be hard-pressed to find an ecosystem as abundant as this anywhere else in the eastern United States.

The vast array of life and beauty in the Smoky Mountains reminds us of an important lesson: all of this is tenuous. We can either be the problem or the protector. We can save or we can destroy. The National Park idea has worked until now because enough people have committed to protect forests, mountains, and streams from our own overreaching natures. As weighty and inconceivable as this sounds, these 19,000+ species of living organisms in the Great Smoky Mountains are our responsibility. If we neglect their home and habitat, if we litter the roads or pluck the flowers or deface the trees or feed the bears, it is to our own detriment. Our National Parks, especially the Smokies, will continue to be a safe haven for American wilderness if we choose to appreciate and preserve, to save and savor. Go and enjoy this magnificent treasure that has been set aside just for you!

Bull Elk

Redbud Tree

<MAMA BEAR AND CUBS 18" x 24" Poster art created in 2015 by Michael Korfhage & Joel Anderson

"It's a blessing and a curse to be the most bio-diverse park in the country. Native species as well as exotics thrive here. The reason we have so much diversity is our climate, latitude and range of elevation. When you enter the park here at Gatlinburg you're around 1,400 feet elevation or less and at Cherokee around 2,000 feet, whereas at the top of the mountain you're over 6,000 feet. That's like driving from here to Maine going through all the different habitats and life zones."
— Dale Ditmanson, Park Superintendent, 2004 - 2013

Butterfly Weed

Appalachian Fir Club-moss

Passion Flower Maypop

Christmas Fern

Flame Azalea

White Trillium

Eastern Chipmunk

Raccoon

White Tailed Deer Fawn

Coyote

Great Smoky Mountains National Park Archives

Red Squirrel

Black Bear

"Here in the forests of the Smokies, where well over a hundred kinds of native deciduous trees are to be found, the spectacle challenges description; the writer feels humbled and gropes for words."
— Arthur Stupka, first GSM Park Naturalist

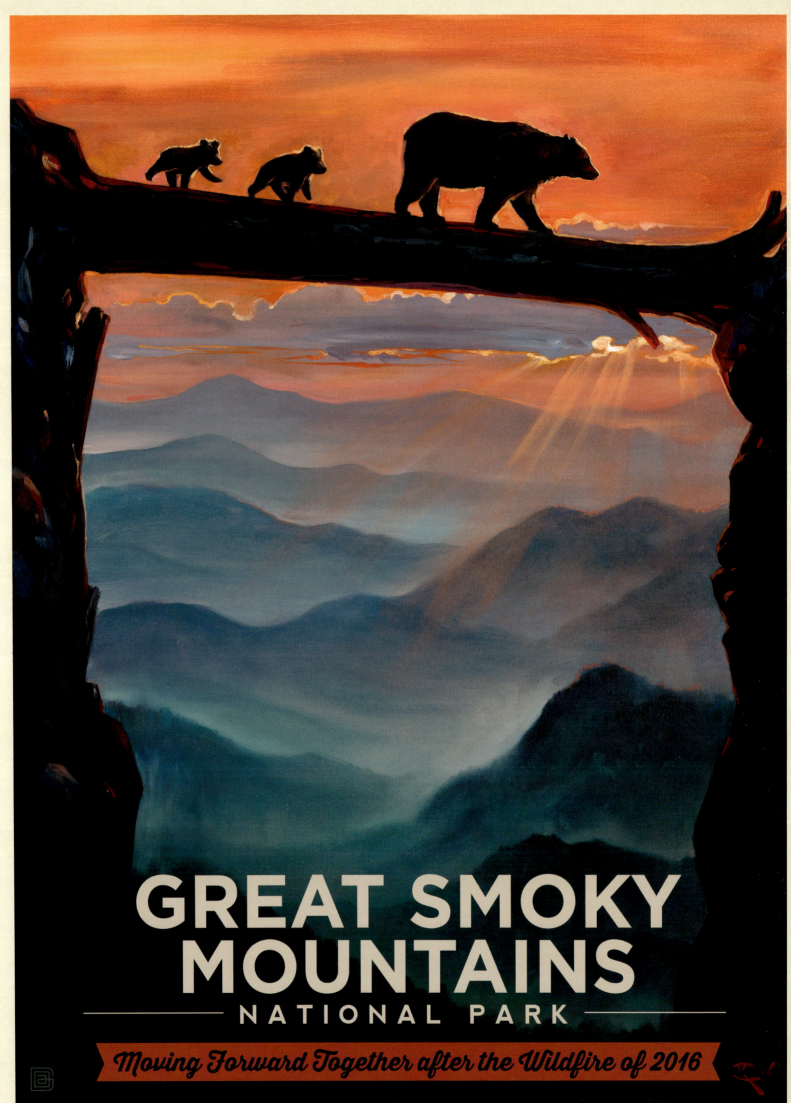

GREAT SMOKY
MOUNTAINS
— NATIONAL PARK —

Moving Forward Together after the Wildfire of 2016

2016 Gatlinburg - Chimney Tops Fire

Photos by Joel Anderson

NATURAL AND HUMAN factors have combined for thousands of years to shape the landscape of the Great Smoky Mountains. A rare convergence of these forces came together on November 28, 2016 to cause the most devastating disaster in the history of Great Smoky Mountains National Park. On that day, a small six-acre fire on Chimney Tops exploded, then roared down the mountain and spread in a matter of hours to over 17,000 acres. It severely damaged or destroyed almost 2,500 structures in the Gatlinburg/Pigeon Forge area, killed 14 people, and injured hundreds more. An estimated 780 firefighters were called in to control the fires from 40 states and the District of Columbia.

In late November 2016, the Smokies were facing one of the most extreme droughts in recent history. Indeed, it had been over four months since the area, traditionally one of the wettest in the United States, had received appreciable rainfall. In addition, fire suppression policies dating back to the early 20th century had eliminated fire from natural forest processes and allowed a fuel load of dead branches and trees to accumulate on the forest floor, making the forest more susceptible to massive fires.

Wildfires were already burning all over the region when a fire began in the underbrush near the peaks of Chimney Tops on Friday, November 25. National Park Service firefighters used standard protocol to combat a wildfire in a remote area inaccessible to firetrucks and motor vehicles, and worked to limit its spread. The fire had expanded to about six acres by Monday, November 28 when conditions became abnormal.

On Monday the 28th, an unusually strong cold front arrived much earlier than officials anticipated blowing hurricane-force winds of up to 90 mph over the Chimney Tops, fanning the wildfire's flames, and blasting embers through the air toward Gatlinburg five miles away. The embers sparked massive conflagrations wherever they landed. In a matter of hours the small fire had spread to over 17,000 acres. Firefighters were quickly overwhelmed and residents and visitors caught unawares had to flee for their lives. Tragically, fourteen individuals perished as a result.

The fire would have been even more devastating had the front which brought the winds not carried heavy rain in its wake. The rains, combined with a massive effort to bring firefighters from all over the country to combat and contain the flames, prevented greater tragedy.

Once the immediate danger had passed, Park officials and local home and business owners were left to assess the damage and begin the recovery process. Because of the nature of the fire, many areas, including the main tourist strip in Gatlinburg, were spared while random areas along the Gatlinburg Spur, Cherokee Orchard Road, Ski Mountain Road, Highway 321 east of town, and Cobbly Knob (ten miles away from Gatlinburg) were devastated.

Volunteers and donations began to pour into the ravaged area and local non-profits organized to provide relief to those affected by the fires. Perhaps most notable were the efforts of local resident, business-owner, philanthropist, and country music superstar Dolly Parton. Through a widely broadcasted telethon and other fundraising activities, the Dollywood Foundation's "My People Fund" raised over $9 million to provide families who lost their homes with up to $1,000 per month for six months. Continuing fundraising efforts are being coordinated by Mountaintough.org.

The Chimney Tops Fire points to several important issues in the Great Smoky Mountains: the power of nature which can never be totally harnessed; the possibility that thoughtless human acts can have devastating consequences; the generosity and resilience of people when faced with disaster; and the responsibility we all have to protect our national treasures.

<BEAR CROSSING: WILDFIRE RELIEF PRINT 18" x 24" Poster created in 2016 by Joel Anderson to raise funds for Gatlinburg fire victims. Based on an original oil painting by Kai Carpenter.

How the Art is Made...

WE WORK AS A TEAM of artists. As founder of Anderson Design Group, I (Joel) have had the great pleasure of collaborating with creative friends to achieve artistic feats that none of us could accomplish alone. I was trained as an illustrator, so when possible, I enjoy rendering a poster from start to finish. But for this project, the best way to produce 40 Smoky Mountain posters along with a book in less than a year was to act like the conductor of a chamber orchestra and write parts for each of my virtuoso players to perform. I started by creating a list of poster themes. Then I assigned illustrations to individual artists who have differing strengths in drawing, painting, and designing in a 20th-Century style. During the process, all five of us were working on different posters at the same time. I would look at progress sketches and renderings each day, offer input and guidance, and then try to stay out of the way as much as possible. As soon as one of the illustrations was turned in, I would spend several more hours adding finishing touches to create continuity with the entire series of posters. This team of artists included long-time collaborator Michael Korfhage, staff artist Aaron Johnson, oil painter Kai Carpenter, and intern-turned-full-time staff artist Derek Anderson. Here is a behind-the-scenes look at how we worked together to create the poster art that fills the pages of this book...

   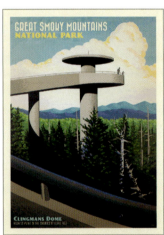

1. *I sketch out the basic composition on the canvas and start blocking in rough color.*
2. *I usually work for 2-3 hours at a time (that's 3-4 of my favorite Tom Petty albums).*
3. *After the main composition and color palette are established, I add smaller details.*
4. *Working in acrylics allows me to work fast, since the paint dries within half an hour.*
5. *Once I am satisfied with a painting, I shoot a high-resolution photo and add type and extra touches in Photoshop.*

JOEL ANDERSON is an illustrator, designer, author and Creative Director. The founder of Anderson Design Group was born in Denver, Colorado and spent his childhood living in places like Curacao, El Salvador, Texas, New York, South Carolina and Florida. He studied illustration at Ringling School of Art & Design. Joel draws on a variety of influences for his work, notably 20th-Century travel poster art and advertising art as well as American folk art. When he is not traveling to take reference photos for books or illustrated poster art, Joel enjoys mentoring and training up-and-coming artists who often become collaborators or full-time staff.

1. Aaron does a rough sketch that shows his vision for the concept and composition.
2. As a digital painter, he roughs in the parts on different layers in Photoshop.
3. Using brushes and textures that he creates to mimic oil painting, Aaron adds detail to the scene.
4. After adding all the detail and experimenting with color, he finishes the scene with accents of fall foliage.

AARON JOHNSON graduated from Watkins School of Art, Design & Film in Nashville, TN. He worked as an intern before joining ADG as a staff artist. Aaron prefers to draw and paint on a tablet hooked up to an iMac computer. Using the same techniques and motions that he would normally use with pencils and brushes, his digital workspace allows for unlimited editing and experimentation with no paint to clean up afterwards! Aaron enjoys making art in different styles, and he can do anything from paintings and WPA era posters, to Art Nouveau and even comic book art.

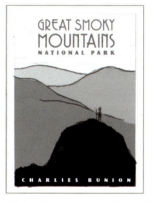

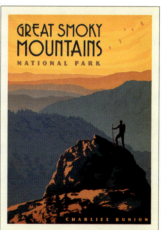

Michael's process and techniques are very similar to Aaron's. He starts with a pencil sketch and then moves to the computer to render his art digitally. Like the rest of us, he is also a fan of old-school poster and advertising art from the early to mid-20th Century.

MICHAEL KORFHAGE works in Nashville as a free-lance illustrator and commercial artist. After graduating from Watkins College of Art, Design & Film, he started collaborating with us as an independent contractor helping me produce poster art. We love working with him because, after working together on more than 100 posters, he knows exactly what we are looking for. Michael also works for magazines, ad agencies, and small businesses. His work is inspired by folk art, mid-century design, and storytelling.

1. I supply photo reference I've shot to share my vision for the poster composition.
2. Derek does more research and expands the idea with a computer-rendering.
3. Once we are both happy with the composition, he begins rendering the illustration.
4. Derek adds typography and finishing touches to the composition. The finished poster design is ready for publication.

DEREK ANDERSON graduated from Watkins School of Art, Design & Film in Nashville, TN. He worked as an intern before joining ADG as a staff artist. Even though he shares the same last name as the company he works for, Derek is not actually related to Joel Anderson—but you wouldn't know that by how much his style fits the Anderson Design Group look! Like his studio mate Aaron, Derek likes to design and illustrate on the computer.

   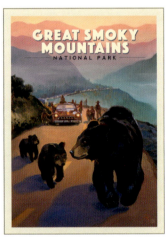

1. After Kai and I discuss the theme, he creates some sketches to establish the direction.
2. Once he transfers his sketch to canvas, he begins painting with oils, roughing in color.
3. As soon as the painting is dry enough to be handled, Kai takes it to a photographer to have a digital photo made.
4. I add some subtle changes in Photoshop to create an area for the typography which I overlay to finish the poster.

KAI CARPENTER grew up in the Pacific Northwest, and works from his Seattle studio. Joel still recalls the first time he saw his work: "I felt like I was looking at magazine cover art from the 1930s or '40s. Kai's style and sense of lighting gives his art a look from a bygone era. I knew his paintings would be a great fit for the vintage-style poster series I was creating." A graduate of the Rhode Island School of Design, Kai has illustrated for numerous clients including Wizards of the Coast and Harper Collins. Kai draws his inspiration from artists of the late 1800s to the 1940s, particularly the Golden Age illustrators.

These are some of Kai Carpenter's pencil sketches that served to establish the concept and composition of each finished oil painting.

More About Anderson Design Group...

IN 1993 I co-founded a design firm to provide for my growing family. For the first decade, we worked mostly on CD and toy packaging, book covers and logos. In 2003, I began creating poster art and training my interns and staff artists to emulate classic poster art styles from the 1920s, '30s and '40s. Our first poster series was the *Spirit of Nashville* collection—a series of prints that celebrated the history and charm of our hometown. Over time, Anderson Design Group morphed into an illustration and design studio with a poster shop on the ground floor. In 2010, after producing over 150 different Nashville designs, I began work on a new series of posters called *The Art & Soul of America*. This was to be a travel poster collection full of my favorite American cities, parks and historical sites. It started out as a small collection of illustrated prints depicting cities like Seattle, New Orleans, New York and Chicago. The prints were a big hit, and I began receiving requests from all over the USA for new art depicting other places that were special to people—places where history or memories were made.

After creating over 200 different prints of U.S. cities and National Parks, I began experimenting with more diverse poster themes like World Travel prints, a coastal collection, posters about coffee, beer and wine, Mid-Century Modern designs, poster art for children, Southern expressions, vintage Americana advertising art, and even a Man Cave collection. By late 2015, the talented artists of Anderson Design Group had helped me produce over 600 different poster designs. And we have since gone global. Our art has been exhibited on every continent on the globe (except for Antarctica). Our prints have been featured on movie and network TV sets, given as gifts to diplomats, hung in embassies and consulates, published in design journals, and displayed in homes and offices by poster art lovers everywhere.

What started in Nashville as a way to celebrate Music City and promote our little Nashville-based design firm has grown to become one of the largest bodies of decorative poster art ever assembled by one team of artists. Now at over 1,000 posters, our collection

is still growing, and it's all available in the Anderson Design Group Studio Store located at 116 29th Ave. North, Nashville, TN 37203, or online at **www.ADGstore.com.**

IN 2016 we finished a massive project—a complete collection of prints celebrating all 59 of the National Parks. We did this to celebrate the Centennial of the National Park Service. In the process, we produced over 150 different illustrated posters and paintings, many of which were included in a special 100th Anniversary coffee table book. The book is available in most National Park Visitor Center gift stores around the USA.

People who enjoy our art often ask us which of the posters are our favorites. The designs that depict parks I have visited with my family rank highest. Like me, folks hang our prints to commemorate a special trip they took with someone they love. Our prints help to freeze a favorite moment in time so people can treasure a special experience forever.

A portion of our annual profits are donated to the National Park Foundation, as well as to groups that support the parks. We love hearing about all the different ways our art is used to protect, promote and preserve our American heritage of Wilderness and Wonder. Feel free to let us know how you are enjoying the art we are so passionate about creating! You can contact us at: **support@andersondesigngroup.com**

Joel Anderson sketching in his Nashville studio

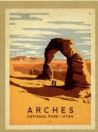
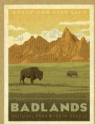

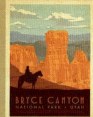
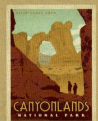
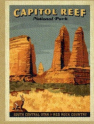

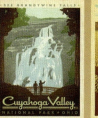
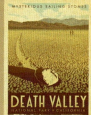

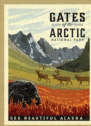

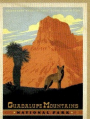

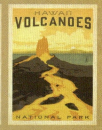

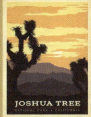
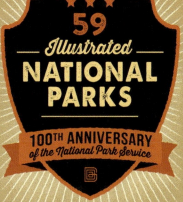

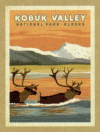

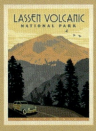

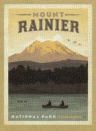
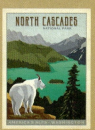

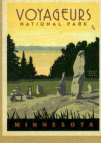

Epilogue

WE HOPE you've enjoyed our Illustrated Guide to Great Smoky Mountains National Park. Beyond your enjoyment, however, we hope this book will stimulate your love and commitment to both the Great Smokies and to America's National Parks. The three of us have come to this work with three core beliefs:

1. The National Parks are without doubt one of America's greatest legacies.

2. As with all great legacies, we, as the recipients of this gift, have a responsibility to be good stewards: to care for and preserve our Parks.

3. And perhaps our greatest responsibility is to expose the next generation of Americans to the beauties and joys of our National Parks, to emphasize the ongoing need to protect them, and instill a desire to preserve them.

The legacy of our National Parks began at an unlikely time in U.S. history. By the end of the 1800s, many Americans believed the nation's natural bounty and beauty were inexhaustible and could be wastefully exploited. Industry was king, and no field, mountain, or stream seemed out of reach. A balance was necessary for our wilderness to survive, and people like John Muir, President Theodore Roosevelt, and Stephen Mather convinced Americans that there were certain places that needed to be preserved inviolate, especially during an era of industrial success.

The Great Smoky Mountains have had their own "voices of those crying out in the wilderness." Horace Kephart, Anne and Willis Davis, David Chapman, George Masa, John D. Rockefeller, Jr., Harvey Broome, and many others not only saw the need to wrest the Smokies from industry's power, but they were willing to sacrifice their time and treasure to make it happen. Indeed, it was the willingness of so many people to contribute their pennies, dimes, and dollars (by the tens, by the thousands, and even by the millions in the case of Rockefeller and the States of Tennessee and North Carolina) to make the Great Smoky Mountains National Park dream a reality. And the sacrifice was not just

Photo by Lydia Pierce

> "It is one of the blessings of wilderness life that it shows us how few things we need in order to be perfectly happy."
> — *Horace Kephart*

monetary; it should never be forgotten that the creation of the Park came at the expense of thousands of mountain residents who were forced to sell their land and move out of their beloved mountains.

As heirs of this great sacrificial gift, we now have a tremendous responsibility as stewards. While we think of National Parks as places where nature rules, human action has a great influence on shaping them. Parks don't protect themselves. We must encourage our government officials to do everything in their power to invest in the future health of our Parks. And no deed is too small. Something as simple as picking up a discarded water bottle on the side of a trail, giving wildlife space while we watch, "leaving no trace" when we camp or backpack are all ways we can continue this legacy of preservation.

Finally, we believe in the need to pass on our love for the Parks to the next generation. Some of our fondest memories growing up were out in nature with our families. As artists and authors, these memories have inspired us beyond measure: standing in breathless awe at the edge of the Grand Canyon; trout fishing in a secluded valley at Glacier; watching our children run across the old church grounds at Oconaluftee; sitting beside golden wildflowers at the foot of the Tetons; splashing through the Narrows at Zion. How could we not want the next generation to know and appreciate these soul-feeding experiences?

The National Park Service has recently made great strides towards promoting the Parks to communities who have not traditionally enjoyed them. We can help this cause by exposing all Americans, no matter their differences in race, ethnicity, or background, to their wilderness birthright. We hope the posters, pictures, and text in this book will inspire you to enjoy and treasure the Great Smoky Mountains and to share your passion for America's National Parks with others.

We wish to dedicate this book with love to our children: Nathan, David, Benji, Mimi, and Esther Anderson and Anna Clare, Taylor, Sully, and Coulter Pierce.